Ætatis suæ 40
THE TRVE PORTRAICT OF CAP: THOMAS IAMES
Some has a time

AF248990

# The Strange and Dangerous Voyage of Capt. Thomas James

Edited and Annotated by W.A. Kenyon

 RŎM
Royal Ontario Museum
Toronto, Canada

© Royal Ontario Museum, 1975

ISBN 0-88854-171-6

Design: John Grant, Information Services, ROM

Photography: James Chambers

Printed and bound in Canada by John Deyell on 80-lb. Georgian Offset Smooth, with 11-point Times Roman type

*To Bill Anderson,*
*Fort Albany, Ontario*

# Preface

Editing *The Strange and Dangerous Voyage of Captain Thomas James* was a time-consuming but delightful task. To sort out the convoluted seventeenth-century syntax and punctuation was no simple matter. On the other hand, there were very few passages where the meaning was obscure, once the syntax had been sorted out. The endless sorting and re-arranging of phrases and adjectives was, by and large, a pleasant task because of the vitality of James' prose. He was a good writer. He was also a product of his age, however, and tended to that literary exuberance which we usually associate with the Elizabethans. This I have muted, or toned down, to make the narrative more acceptable to the modern ear and sensibilities. I also substituted modern words in those places where James' meaning was clear, but where the word he used to express that meaning has since taken on a new connotation. For example, he consistently used the word "discovery" where we would use the word "exploration"; I have substituted the modern word in all such instances. I have also annotated James' text wherever I felt that editorial comments would lead to increased clarity.

James was also a master mariner who paid constant attention to wind, weather, tide and soundings. Some of these details, particularly tidal data, I have simply deleted because they seemed to clutter up the narrative without adding anything significant to the story.

The reader who wishes to pursue the study of Thomas James might consult the following: Miller Christy's edition of *The Voyages of Captain Luke Foxe of Hull, and Captain Thomas James of Bristol In Search of a North-West Passage, in 1631–32*, published by The

Hakluyt Society, London, 1894, and the article on Thomas James by Alan Cooke in the *Dictionary of Canadian Biography*. The Hakluyt Society edition of James' *Strange and Dangerous Voyage* was used in preparing the present work.

In the overall preparation of this manuscript I have been ably assisted by my secretary, Miss Peta Daniels. The endless typing of manuscripts was done by Mrs. Myra Colby and Miss Margaret Coutinho. Field photographs were taken by Mr. James A. Chambers, Photography Department, Royal Ontario Museum. Maps were redrawn by Mrs. Georgina Hosek, Royal Ontario Museum, and apart from that of James himself, were provided by the Map Division, Public Archives of Canada. James' map, as well as his portrait, are published through the courtesy of the Hakluyt Society. Studio photographs were taken by the Photography Department, Royal Ontario Museum.

W.A.K.
Office of the Chief Archaeologist, ROM
July 1974

# Contents

# List of Plates



# List of Maps

# Introduction

Charlton is a small, uninhabited island nestled in the southeast corner of James Bay. If you fly over it in one of the small float-planes that make northern travel so delightful, you feel that you are looking down into a park, completely surrounded by broad, shallow tidal flats and reefs. If you examine it more closely, you see that there is a flat-topped ridge or plateau rising abruptly from the north-east point of the island, and stretching westward for two or three miles; near the southeast corner of the island is a similar ridge. Apart from these ridges, which rise little more than 100 feet above sea-level, the island is a low, undulating, sandy plain, liberally dotted with small, shallow lakes. Although there are fairly dense stands of spruce around most of the ponds, and along most of the streams, much of the island consists of open parkland and meadows, sprinkled with just the occasional evergreen.

The major axis of the island, running from the northeast to the southwest point, is some 17 or 18 miles long. On the east side of Charlton, a broad, shallow bay is protected on the south by Danby Island, and on the east by Cary Island. From the bottom of the bay, you can see a narrow channel leading to a large slough or pond that is known locally as Salt Water Lake. At low tide, the pilot will tell you, there is such a small trickle of water flowing through the channel that it is possible for a determined person with an affinity for mud to walk across it with relative ease. At high tide, there is just enough water over the bar to float a small freight-canoe.

If you wish to examine the island more closely, you must ask the pilot to put you ashore; and only then do you realize how extensive

the surrounding reefs really are. For he will land the plane only in
the narrow channel between Charlton and Danby islands, and put
you ashore only at House Point, where a long-abandoned Hudson's
Bay Company depot now stands. Built around the turn of the century, the depot was a warehouse for the goods that were brought
into James Bay by boat. From there, they were delivered to the
various trading posts on the mainland by smaller vessels that were
kept in the bay for that purpose. When the railroad from the south
reached James Bay in 1932, it was no longer profitable to use the
old route through Hudson Strait, so the depot was closed. All that
remains today is a handful of abandoned buildings—the old staff-
house, the district manager's house, and the gas-house. Over the
door of the latter, a badly weathered sign warns the curious, in both
English and Cree, that smoking is not permitted in that area.

Wandering inland from the old depot, you find that the park-land
you noticed from the air, and indeed the entire island, is composed
of a fine, white sand, covered with a thick, spongy carpet of caribou-
moss. Blueberries and strawberries are scattered about with incredible profusion; cranberries and saskatoon berries, though not so pro-
lific, are still quite plentiful. It is an odd sensation—at least for a
southerner—to stretch out on the moss on a warm, sunny afternoon,
and be enveloped with the sweet, sticky smell of crushed berries. As
you lie there you suddenly realize that Charlton Island is a strangely
muted place. The geese and ducks that nest all over it are quiet and
unobtrusive, as though they were reluctant to announce their
presence till their young ones are old enough to fly. The loons are
a bit more boisterous, but only if they are well off shore. At home,
they too are silent. Beaver are plentiful on the ponds and streams,
but they go quietly and industriously about their business. On
bare patches of sand, or along the beach, the tracks of foxes and
lynx will frequently appear, though the animals themselves are
neither seen nor heard. There is nothing to mark their passing but
the line of their footprints. If you follow their tracks, you find that
they never deviate from their fixed path. Never do they stop to see
if there might be some tasty or intriguing object lurking behind a
boulder, or beneath a fallen log. They clearly have some urgent
and personal matters to attend to on the other side of the island.

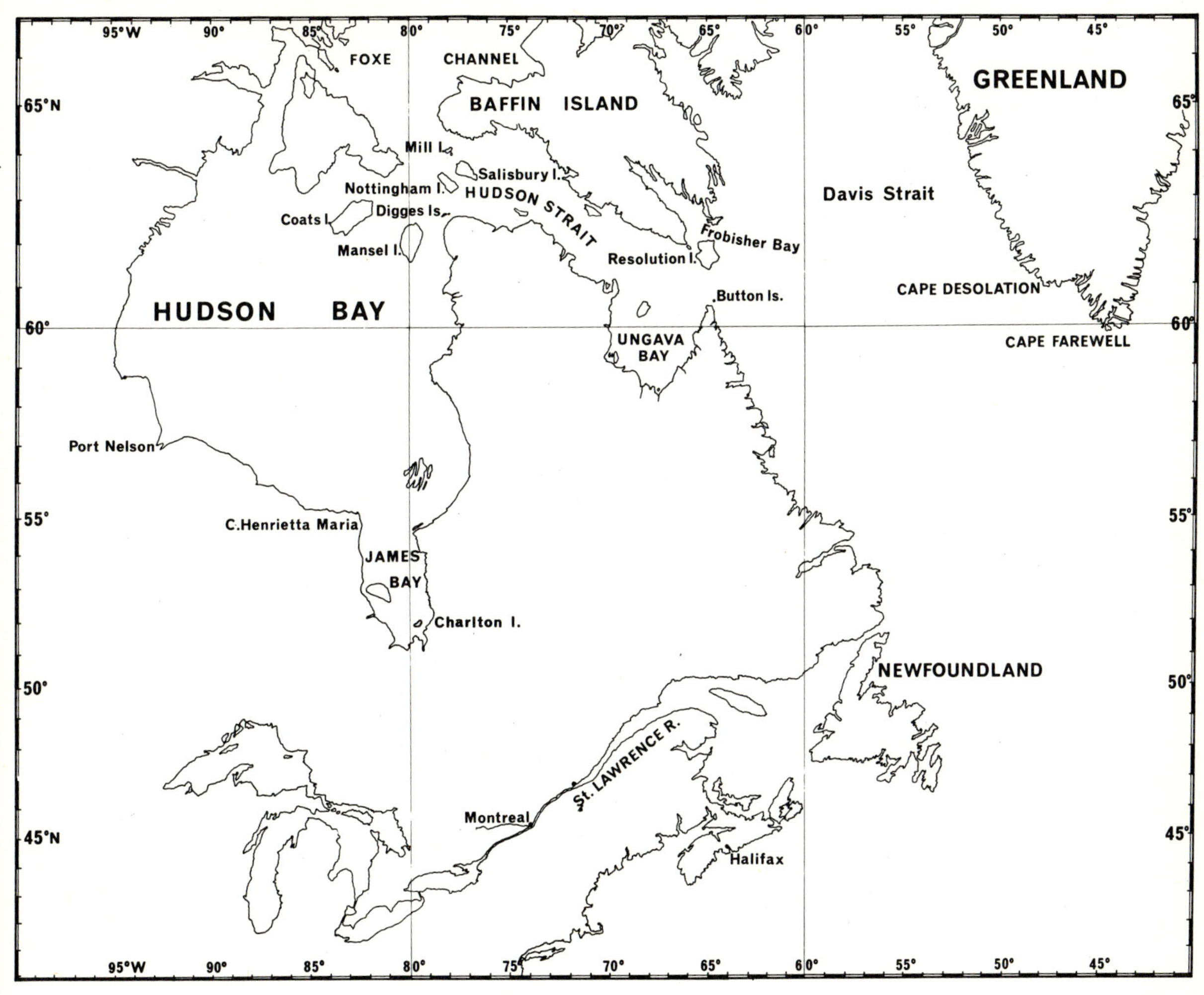


Map 1  Northeastern North America

As you continue your explorations, your impressions gradually sort themselves out. You reach a point, finally, where you are no longer bothered by the apparent contradiction between the feeling of silence and solitude on the one hand, and the richness and vitality of the living things on the other. For you know that in some distant valley, near the beginning of time, another explorer must have felt the same way as he set out one evening to stroll through *his* garden, thoughtfully munching an apple.

Charlton Island was named by Captain Thomas James, who spent the winter of 1631–32 near the northeast point of the island. James had been selected by the Society of Merchant Venturers of Bristol, England, to search for the northwest passage leading to the Orient, a search that had started fifty-five years earlier with the first voyage of Martin Frobisher. The Bristol merchants had been prodded into activity by a group of London merchants who had petitioned King Charles I for permission to send a ship in search of the northwest passage. The king not only granted permission for the venture, but offered the London merchants the use of one of his own ships, the *Charles*. What the Bristol merchants feared was that the London group would be granted a monopoly on trade through the northwest passage if they were lucky enough, or skilful enough, to locate that elusive gateway to the riches of the Orient. They proposed, therefore, that the Bristol merchants, too, be permitted to send a ship to the northwest, and that trading privileges be granted to both groups if the passage were actually discovered.

With royal approval, matters moved rapidly forward. Captain Luke Fox had already been appointed commander of the *Charles,* when Captain Thomas James of Bristol was chosen to command that city's vessel, the 70-ton *Henrietta Maria* which was named after England's queen. We know almost nothing about the vessel, apart from the incidental clues which James left us in his narrative. As we put these clues together, however, it is obvious that it was a typical vessel of the era. It set a sprit-sail, a fore-sail and fore top-sail, a main-sail and main top-sail, and a lateen sail on the mizzen. This had been



standard rig for the smallest men-of-war and for most merchantmen

since the early 1500s, and was to continue till the introduction of
jibs in the early eighteenth century. The vessel had two decks, an
upper and lower, with hatches leading into the hold from the lower
or orlop deck. In the hold itself, there was a bread-room and a
powder-room, as well as storage space for the supplies that were
required to keep both vessel and crew in operation. The bread-room
would normally be located astern, and the powder-room in the
bows. On the orlop deck, the one immediately above the hold, the
gun-room was situated in the stern and lay above the bread-room
and below the great cabin on the upper deck.

The *Maria* had a total complement of 22 people, the same number
that sailed aboard Luke Fox's ship, the *Charles*. James' crew-list
has not survived, but in his journal he refers to all of his officers by
name at one time or another. Thus we are able to draw up the
following roster:

| | |
|---|---|
| Captain | Thomas James |
| Lieutenant | William Clements |
| Master | Arthur Price |
| First Mate | John Warden |
| Second Mate | John Whittered |
| Boatswain | John Palmer |
| Gunner | Richard Edwards |
| Gunner's Mate | John Barton |

We know, in addition, that the surgeon's name was Nathaniel Bilson, and that the carpenter was William Cole. A cooper is mentioned on several different occasions, but his name is not recorded.
Nor do we know the name of the cook who spent the winter steeping
his beef in a large tub, boiling down the broth, then adding oatmeal
to make a thick, hot gruel for the men. George Ugganes and David
Hammon are both mentioned, but only incidentally. Presumably
they were common sailors.

There is a great temptation, at this point, to launch into a detailed
examination of life aboard the *Henrietta Maria*. How, for example,
did James find his way across the north Atlantic? How were meals
prepared aboard ship? We know the answers to these and similar

questions, but rightly or wrongly, I have decided to leave them in abeyance. I have decided to pare my introductory remarks to the barest minimum that is consistent with understanding. For Captain Thomas James is quite capable of telling his own story.

James sailed from Bristol about three o'clock in the afternoon on May 3rd, 1631. Raising the coast of Greenland on June 4th, he beat his way around Cape Farewell, then sailed up the west coast to Cape Desolation at 60° north latitude. From there he sailed west, half a point north, to pick up the southern tip of Resolution Island, where he arrived on June 18th. Because of ice and bad weather, it took him almost a month to beat his way through Hudson Strait. Passing finally between Digges Island and Nottingham Island, he swung to the southwest till he reached Mansell Island, and from there sailed across Hudson Bay to the west coast, which he sighted on August 11th. He then coasted along the western and southern shores of the bay till he reached Cape Henrietta Maria, which he named after the queen—and his ship—on September 2.

Until he arrived at the mouth of the Nelson River, James was sailing in known waters, even though they had not been explored in any detail. Sir Thomas Button had spent the winter of 1612–13 at the mouth of the Nelson, which he had named after the master of his ship, the *Discovery*. Seven years later, the Danish explorer, Jens Munk, had wintered at the mouth of the Churchill River. But once he had passed the Nelson, James was on his own. He knew, of course, that Henry Hudson and his crew had spent the winter of 1610-11 somewhere to the southeast, but for all practical purposes, Hudson's surviving map was useless. James tried to continue following the coast when it swung to the south around the cape, but it was getting late in the season, and the weather was deteriorating rapidly. After he had spent a month wandering in and out of the maze of islands, shoals and reefs that stretches down the whole east side of the bay, he found himself in Charlton Sound.

On October 3rd, 1631, James landed for the first time on the island where he was destined to spend the winter, and which he later named Charlton. On internal evidence in his narrative, we know

that he anchored his ship just to the south of the reef that stretches
eastward from the northeast point of the island. We know, too, that
the three small buildings in which he spent the winter, and which
he named Charles Town in honour of Charles, Prince of Wales,
were built below the high bluff which rises from that same point.

Throughout the long and bitter winter, James looked to the physical
and emotional welfare of his men. Against the ravages of scurvy, he
could do very little, but both he and the surgeon did what they
could to make the men comfortable. In the spring, they managed—
almost miraculously—to repair their battered ship; and by July 2nd,
1632, the ice was sufficiently dispersed that they could continue
their exploration. There was really very little that they could do,
however, except to feel their way cautiously north, along the west
side of the bay, and thus into more familiar waters. He then retraced
his route of the previous year till he reached Nottingham Island.
From there, he tried to penetrate northward into what we know
today as Fox Basin, but the passage was hopelessly choked with ice.
When they reached an estimated latitude of 65° 30′ north, James
and his officers discussed their position, and agreed that they should
head for England. On September 3rd they were at Resolution
Island, and pushing out into the broad Atlantic swells.

When Captain James returned to Bristol on October 22nd, 1632,
he was received with every mark of respect by the Merchant Venturers who had sent him into Hudson Bay to search for the northwest passage. They accepted without question his statement that
there was no passage leading from Hudson Bay to the Pacific Ocean.
Nor did they question his opinion that if any northwest passage did
exist, it was above 66° north latitude, and would therefore prove
worthless as a commercial route to the fabulous wealth of the south
seas. Within two weeks of his return, James was on his way to London with letters from the Merchant Venturers to some of their
influential friends at court. The letters requested that an audience
be arranged so that James could tell his story directly to King
Charles. During the audience, which lasted for two hours, the king
was both gracious and curious. He examined the map of the voyage
which James presented to him, asked many questions and arranged

for the publication of James' journal with all possible dispatch.

When it appeared in early March of the following year, *The Strange and Dangerous Voyage,* by Captain Thomas James, was an immediate success, and its author continued to bask in the royal favour; this, combined with the fame that was generated by his exploits, made him a very popular figure in London's social and political circles. That James was both very popular and widely respected is beyond any serious doubt. Yet he did not allow his popularity to interfere with the business at hand. For some two months after the publication of his journal he was appointed commander of one of His Majesty's Ships of the Line, the *9th Whelp of the Lion,* with orders to assist in suppressing the pirates who infested Bristol Channel and the Irish Sea. James was recommended for promotion in October, 1633, when his superior, the Earl of Stafford, Lord Deputy of Ireland, informed the Lords of the Admiralty that he was diligent, civil in his conversation, and an able man in his profession. But he did not live to be rewarded with the rapid promotion that would surely have been his. He died in 1635, at about 42 years of age; he left all his worldly goods to his one surviving sister, and was probably buried in the Lord Mayor's Chapel in Bristol.

In spite of the widespread popularity that he enjoyed during his lifetime, James is generally held in rather low esteem today. He is still accepted as a scholarly and kindly man, for both his scholarship and his concern for the welfare of his crew are clearly evident in his journal. And the comprehensive list of navigational instruments that he assembled, all fashioned to his own exacting specifications, shows that he was thoroughly acquainted with the most recent developments in the theory and practice of navigation. This is borne out, too, by the remarkable accuracy of his observations when he had a reasonably stable platform from which to take his sights. To give but one example, he located his wintering place on Charlton Island at 52° 03′ north, which, for all practical purposes, is dead on. If James' technical and personal qualifications were as unassailable as they appear to be, then how are we to account for the lack of esteem in which he is currently held? (For a popular contemporary evaluation of James, see "Captain James: Fool or Hero?", by

Harold W. Helfrich, Jr., *The Beaver*, Summer 1972, pp. 42–45.)

If we examine the criticisms that have been levelled at James over
the years, we find that they fall rather neatly into three categories:
(1) his refusal to hire any crew member who had had previous
Arctic experience; (2) the frightful gamble which he took when he
deliberately sank his ship with very poor odds that it could ever be
raised to sail again; (3) his apparent tendency to exaggeration. Let
us look, then, at these charges. The refusal of James to take any
experienced people with him is usually interpreted as an indication
of megalomania, and is frequently cited as the cause of many of his
difficulties. Certainly James is explicit on the subject. He summarily
rejected all "Voluntary Loyterers," and announced that men would
be hired only if they were "Unmarried, Approved, Able, and
Healthy." He apparently had no trouble in finding men who met his
specifications, for he tells us that "in a few days, an abundant number presented themselves, furnished with general sufficiency in
Marine Occasions." Many people with experience in northern
waters did apply, but he flatly refused to consider anyone "that had
been in the like Voyage, or Adventurers, for some private Reasons
unnecessary here to be related; keeping thus the Power in my own
Hands, I had all the men to acknowledge *immediate Dependence*
upon my self alone; both for Direction and Disposing of all, as well
of the Navigation, as all other things whatsoever."

That James insisted on keeping direction and control of every phase
of the expedition in his own hands might indeed suggest megalomania. I suspect, however, that his unusual behaviour may reflect
nothing more irregular than a concern over the possibility of mutiny.
And under the circumstances, that was a possibility which any alert
commander would surely have considered when planning a search
for the northwest passage. For it was just 20 years since Robert
Bylot had sailed Henry Hudson's ship, the *Discovery,* from Hudson
Bay back to England, bringing with him the seven other members
of the party who had survived. James knew of the mutiny aboard
the *Discovery*. He knew that Henry Hudson, his son, and six members of the crew had been cast adrift in a small boat somewhere in
the southeast portion of what is now James Bay. He knew, also, that

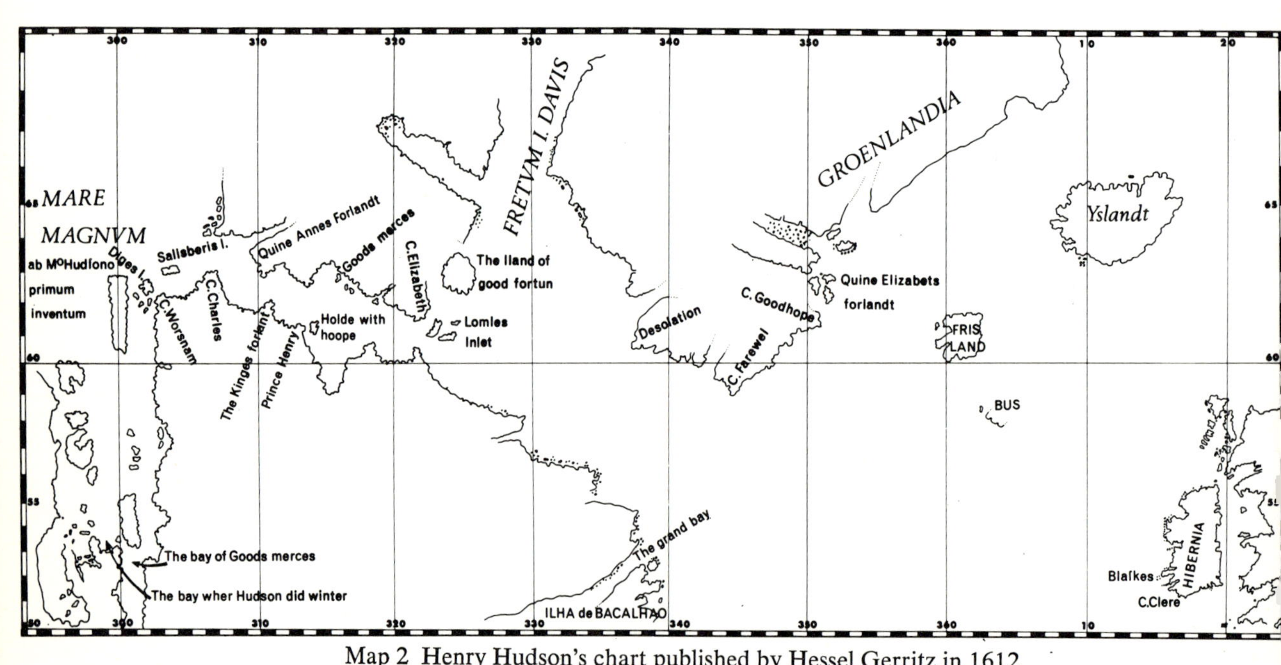


Map 2  Henry Hudson's chart published by Hessel Gerritz in 1612

three of the mutineers had been killed by the Eskimo on Digges
Island, and that another had died at sea during the return voyage.
Knowing all this, James probably decided that the only way he
could be sure of avoiding a mutiny was to make himself indispen-
sable: he would avoid Hudson's fate by making certain that he was
the only member of the crew who could sail the ship back to
England.

The second charge is more difficult to deal with, because so little is
known about James' earlier career. He was an experienced sea-
captain and navigator, but we cannot be certain that he, himself,
had actually had Arctic experience. My own feeling is that the
1631–32 expedition was not the first voyage that he had made to the
Arctic, and that his decision to sink his ship, the *Henrietta Maria,*
was a reasoned decision based on experience—uncomfortable
though it surely was. On the first page of his journal, during a discussion of the preparations for the voyage, he tells us that "a great
Ship (as by former Experience I had found) was unfit to be forc'd
thorow the ice. ..." Although generations of scholars and writers
have tried to figure out what James meant by the phrase that he
himself enclosed in parentheses, it probably means exactly what it
says, that he had previous experience in Arctic waters. If this is true,
it places the entire matter in a different light, for then James would
know precisely what his options were.

In his introduction to the Hakluyt Society edition of the voyage of
Thomas James, Miller Christy, the editor, made the following
observation, "it is difficult," he said, "to understand how it can have
been really necessary to adopt the extraordinary expedient of sinking the ship in order to preserve her." Christy fails to say, however,
what he thinks James should have done, or what he, himself, would
have done in a similar situation. Nor did he know, apparently, that
James' actions were not particularly unusual; Martin Frobisher,
for example, had sunk a pinnace in the Countess of Warwick's
Sound in 1577, "minding to have him againe the next yeare."

Ideally, James should have pulled his ship up on shore for the
winter and launched her again after break-up in the spring. Lacking

facilities for that, he should have wintered her in some sheltered bay or cove, or in the mouth of a small creek, anywhere that she would be protected from storms and the irresistible pressure of ice during spring break-up. James actually spent the month of September looking for a suitable place to winter his ship, but none was to be found. Cruising up and down the bay with increasing desperation, he finally found himself trapped by the onset of winter in the wide shallow bay on the east end of what he later named Charlton Island.

And now that he could look no farther, what was he to do with his ship? If he left her at anchor out in the bay, she would be exposed both to storms and to strong tidal currents. Even if she survived a winter in the ice, she could not possibly survive the spring break-up. For then she would be seized by the ice and swept to certain destruction in the maze of shoals and reefs that surrounded her. James could at least minimize that danger by moving his ship out of the main sweep of the tidal current, and into the shallows along the shore. But there he was threatened by the surf that he knew would be raised by either a north, northeast or east wind. And any vessel caught in the surf would be broken up by the constant, rhythmic pounding on the bottom. James had already moved the *Henrietta Maria* out of the main tidal stream, and into shoal water as close to shore as he dared to bring her when the wind shifted to the east. As he had feared, the vessel began to pound viciously in the rising surf, and as a last resort, she was scuttled. There was nothing else he could do.

The final criticism levelled at Thomas James is his apparent tendency towards exaggeration. Sir John Barrow, for example, said that James' journal was largely a lamentation, weeping and great mourning—and there is much substance to that charge. For each wave that James reported tended to become the highest, steepest and most malevolent wave that he had ever seen. Each storm was more fearful than the last; each patch of shoal water was more extensive, rocky and perilous than the one from which they had just escaped. And very often, those terrifying and catastrophic events occurred so close together that there was not even time for the cap-

tain and crew to kneel in prayer, or time to express proper gratitude
for their miraculous deliverance.

Behind the lamentations, however, lay some incredibly bad weather
as well as the ice, fog, and shoal water that make navigation in those
waters a hazardous undertaking even today. On Friday, August
26th, 1910, for example, 300 years after Henry Hudson had first
nosed his little ship, the *Discovery,* through the ice of Hudson and
James bays, a Danish barque, the *Sorine,* arrived off Charlton
Island. She had been chartered in London by the Hudson's Bay
Company to deliver a cargo of merchandise to James Bay. J.M.
Anderson, who was on Charlton Island when the Danish vessel
arrived there, recorded her career in his book, *Fur Trader's Story*:
"Alas," he says, "this was to be the *Sorine's* last voyage. After dis-
charging cargo at Charlton she took on rock ballast and set sail for
the return voyage to England. She ran into some ice in Hudson Bay;
there was a minor mutiny on the part of the crew; and this adverse
concatenation of events forced the captain to return her and run her
aground on Charlton Island for the winter. But winter ice conditions
are not kind to ships in such waters, and the lovely *Sorine* left her
bones at the place named Charles Town by Captain James."

The Strange and Dangerous Voyage
of Capt. Thomas James

# The Preparations to the Voyage

For many years my honourable and worshipful friends had been urging me to undertake a voyage of discovery. They wanted me to locate and explore that part of the world which is commonly called the "Northwest Passage." Through this, I was to sail to the South Sea, cross to Japan and then continue around the world to the westward. They pressed me forward, also, by pointing out that the King's most excellent Majesty would be very pleased with such an undertaking. I finally discussed the matter with my honoured friends, the merchants of Bristol. These men have always supported anyone who followed the paths of virtue, particularly when such activities also led to the enlargement and benefit of His Majesty's Kingdoms. Therefore, they freely offered to finance such an expedition.

With this backing, I approached the Honourable Sir Thomas Roe, Kt., who is one of the most learned and widely travelled men in England today.[1] He gladly presented to His Majesty, Charles I, the willingness of the Bristol Merchants and myself to enter into His Majesty's service in this manner. His Majesty most graciously accepted the offer, and encouraged me in my modest undertaking by many favours. I therefore set to work immediately to organize the expedition, while the merchants raised the necessary funds so that the treasurer would have ready cash to pay for anything I considered necessary for the voyage.

I had thought for a long time that a venture such as we were planning could be carried out most efficiently by a single ship. For two or more ships would certainly become separated in those icy and fog-enshrouded seas, even without the storms and accidents which we would surely encounter. And during a voyage of discovery, a rendezvous would be both uncertain and time-consuming. Because speed and perseverance are the very life of such a venture, I resolved to have but one ship, together with the ship's boat and shallop. Previous experience had taught me that a large ship was unfit to be forced through the ice. I therefore chose a strong, well-built vessel of 70 tons burden, and placed the hopes of my future fortunes in God and that only ship.

I estimated that the voyage would last at least 18 months. Next, I reckoned how much food and other necessary gear the vessel would hold. Finally, I calculated the number of men that these supplies would support for an 18-month voyage at the usual ration, and found that it was 22. This was a small group to carry out such a venture, but double the number required to handle the ship efficiently and safely.

The baker, brewer, butcher and other tradesmen performed most creditably. Indeed, they knew that any failure on their part would lead to their utter undoing because this was a general venture involving many of the Bristol merchants. But they proved themselves to be truly masters of their arts, and have my gratitude for their honest care and the contribution they made to the success of the voyage. Meanwhile the carpenters did everything possible to make the ship strong and serviceable.

With everything properly organized and the size of my crew known, I asked myself what kind of men I wanted, and what abilities they should have. First, I rejected all voluntary loiterers and announced that I would have only unmarried, well-recommended, able and healthy seamen. From these applicants I selected a boatswain with a few assistants to start rigging the ship. While this was being done, I shipped the ordinary seamen. Only when all arrangements were completed did I sign on the mates; and last of all, the master of my ship, and my lieutenant. The whole company were strangers to me and to each other (that is, personally), but yet privately recommended by worthy merchants for their ability and loyalty.

Plate 1  The *Susan Constant*. This replica is the same type as James' ship the *Henrietta Maria* (no drawings extant). Courtesy Jamestown Foundation, Williamsburg, Va.

I was sought out by a number of men who had formerly occupied
positions of the highest authority on similar expeditions, and by
others with general experience in the icy northern seas. But I
rejected them all, refusing to consider anyone with any previous
experience in such matters.[2] This was for personal reasons which
it is not necessary to explain here. Thus I kept all the power in my
own hands, the overall direction of the voyage, the navigation,
and all other things whatsoever.

Meanwhile, to brush up on my navigation, I collected journals,
charts, articles and whatever else might be of assistance. I set skilful
workmen to make me quadrants, staves, semicircles,[3] etc., but did
not permit them to calibrate the instruments, as I distrusted the
hands of a mere mechanic. I had the calibration done by an in-
genious practitioner of mathematics. I likewise had compass-needles
made according to the most reasonable and accurate methods that
could be devised. And by the first of April, everything was ready to
be assembled in our hopeful ship.

In the meantime, I travelled up to London to learn His Majesty's
further pleasure, and to let him know that I was ready to sail. His
Majesty summoned the honourable knight mentioned earlier [Sir
Thomas Roe], and shortly afterwards I received His Majesty's Royal
Letters.[4] Whereupon I moved the ship into the road, waiting only
for a fair wind to begin the voyage.

# A Voyage for the Discovery of a Northwest Passage into the South Sea

The 2nd of May, 1631, I took my leave of the Worshipful Merchant Adventurers in this action, in the city of Bristol; and being accompanied by a Reverend Divine, a Mr. Thomas Palmer, several of the merchants and some relatives and countrymen, I repaired on board. There Mr. Palmer preached a sermon. He exhorted us to maintain brotherly love amongst ourselves, and to dare to profess the true Christian religion wherever our wanderings might lead us. After they had received such entertainment as my estate could afford them, they departed for Bristol. In the afternoon, I checked our supplies—clothes, food, etc.— and arranged for the delivery of some items that were wanting.

Two days later, after prayers for the prosperity and success of our endeavours, we weighed anchor about three o'clock in the afternoon, and stood down the channel of the Severn. Although the winds were light, we slowly worked our way to the west of Lundie. Then the head-winds became so strong that we were forced to bear up, and anchor in Lundie Road on the evening of the 5th. There we remained till the morning of the 8th. Then, hoping that the wind would remain favourable, we again set sail, but were forced to put into Milford, where we anchored about midnight. We remained there till the morning of May 17th; then, with the first favouring wind we got under weigh, and doubled about Cape Cleere in Ireland.

By the 22nd we were at 51° 26′ north, with the Blaskes bearing northeast about 12 leagues away. [The Blaskes are in latitude 52° 4′ north.] There I ordered the course altered to west northwest, if the

variable and unpredictable winds of the area would permit such a
course.

**June, 1631**

The 4th of June we raised the coast of Greenland, in very thick and
foul weather, and stood in close to get our bearings. By two o'clock
the next morning, we found ourselves completely surrounded by
ice. Because visibility was so poor, our attempts to get clear of the
ice actually took us deeper and deeper into the pack. After some
serious and fearful buffeting, we made fast to a large floe, and
worked day and night with poles to ward off drifting cakes of ice
that were being tossed about by the storm.

On the 6th, about two o'clock in the morning, we were beset with
unusually large pieces of ice which came at us with what looked
like a wilful violence. Had we not set some sail, it would doubtless
have crushed us to pieces. In escaping that danger, we ran against
another great floe with such force that we thought our ship had been
stove in; but when we manned the pumps, we found she was still
dry. During our first encounter with the ice, our shallop had been
badly damaged. I therefore had our long-boat brought up from
between decks and put overboard. With her help, we recovered our
broken shallop and hauled it up on deck so that we could rebuild it.

During a gale lasting all that day, we were fearfully beaten by the
ice. In the evening we were surrounded by great pieces as high as
our poop, with their sharp blue corners reaching right under the
ship. Those great pieces pounded us so badly that it was a wonder
the ship could endure even one such blow. It was God, alone, that
did preserve us—to whom be all honour and glory. In this extremity, I had the men set what sail they could, and the ship forced her
way through the ice, though tossed and buffeted worse than any ship
before her. When we were clear of the ice, we manned the pumps
and found her dry. So we knelt in prayer and praised God for our
merciful delivery.

     The 7th and 8th of June we spent beating around Cape Farewell, although we were then still pestered with much ice. By the 9th day, we were 59° north, and some 10 leagues west of the cape. The latitude of the Blaskes in Ireland is 52° 4′ north, and that of Cape Farewell is 59° north. The course is west northwest, and the distance about 410 leagues.[5] I know very well that these latitudes, courses and distances do not agree exactly with mathematical conclusions, but thus we found them to be. The variation of the compass in latitude 52° 30′ north, and 30 leagues west of Ireland is about 3° east. At latitude 57° north, and about 310 leagues west northwest from the Blaskes the compass variation is 9° west. Some 40 leagues east of Cape Farewell, at a latitude of 59° 15′ north, the variation is about 14° 45′. During this voyage, I have kept a careful watch to see if there were any currents that set to the northeast, as is suggested by some earlier writers, but could not detect any. The winds here are variable, and the sea of an unfathomable depth.

Between Ireland and Greenland we did not see any whales or other fish;[6] the weather, for the most part, was foggy and misty, and as wet as rain. The morning of June 10th was very foul, with a heavy sea, and with ice not too far away in any direction—and some pieces as high as our top-mast head. Our long-boat was being towed astern, because we were rebuilding the shallop on deck, when the tow-line suddenly parted, and we had much trouble in recovering her. This we did, however, and finally got her aboard, badly bruised. While heaving her aboard, two men were seriously hurt and almost lost. By eight o'clock in the evening we were as far north as Cape Desolation, for we found the land to trend away north and by east, and thus we knew it to be the cape. It stands at 60° north latitude and is about 40 leagues northwest of Cape Farewell.

The distance from Cape Desolation to the south end of Resolution Island is about 140 leagues, and the course is west, half a point north. The latitude of the south end of the island is 61° 20′ north.[7] Some 12 leagues west of Cape Desolation the variation is 16°. In this course, we were much tormented, pestered and beaten by the ice, many pieces of which were higher than our mast-top head. On our way, we saw so many walruses that the sea seemed full of them. The weather, for the most part, was a stinking fog, with the sea

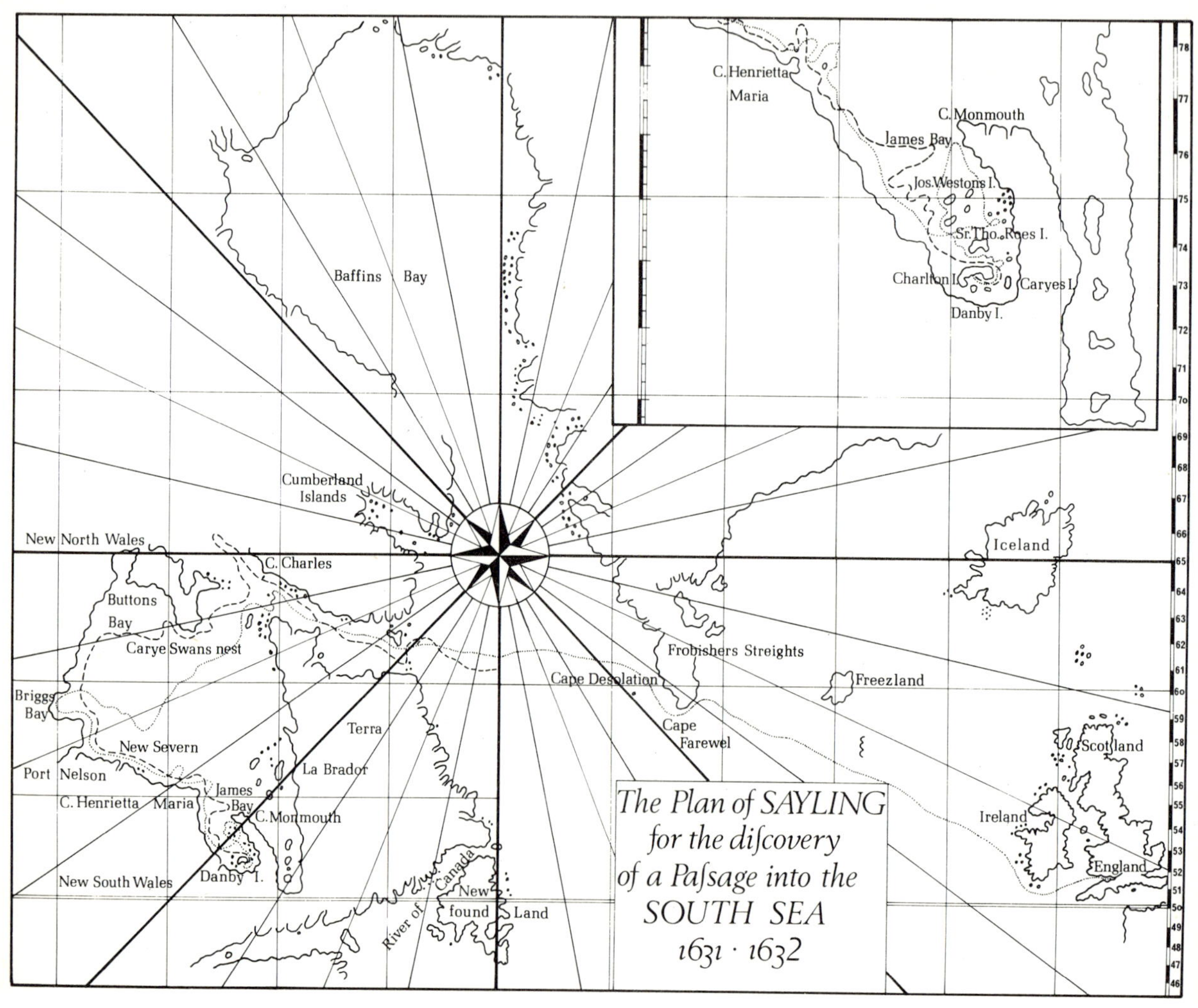


Map 3  Thomas James' map published in 1633

being very black. I believe this blackness is caused by the fog.

During the night of June 17th, we though we heard the surf pounding on the shore; later we learned that it was not the shore but a bank of ice along the shore that the surf was pounding on. It made a hollow and hideous sound, like an overfall of water.[8] At the time, we tried to determine what caused the noise, but could not see anything because the night was so dark and foggy. We stood off from the shore till daybreak, then stood in again; and about four o'clock in the morning, we saw the land rising above the fog, and knew it to be Resolution Island. That night was so cold that our sails and rigging froze.

We endeavoured to beat our way around the southern point of the island but were unsuccessful, for we were terribly pestered by the ice and blinded by a very thick fog. The tide in the strait is very quick, with the ebb as strong as the flood. The fog was of such a piercing nature that it spoiled all our compasses, making them so sluggish and heavy that they wouldn't move. I would therefore advise anyone planning to sail these latitudes in the future to provide themselves with compasses of Muscovia Glass[9], or some other substance that will withstand the moisture of this climate. As the fog cleared up, we could see that the entrance to the strait was choked with ice. When we tried to move through it, we were suddenly trapped, and could do nothing but drift with the pack. Four leagues from shore, we found no bottom at 230 fathoms.

By the morning of June 20th, we had drifted around the southern point of the island, when the wind shifted to the west and drove both us and the ice towards the shore. When we had been driven to within two league of the shore, we found ourselves amongst the strangest whirlings of the sea that could be imagined. There were many icebergs grounded in 40 fathoms of water. Coming out of the broken grounds[10] of the island, and swirling amongst the grounded ice-bergs, the ebb-tide made such a distraction that we were carried with it. Sometimes we were carried almost onto the rocks; at other times we were swept so close to the towering icebergs that we were afraid they would fall over and crush us. Also, we were so bruised

with banging against the ice that our situation was most desperate.
To protect ourselves, I fastened a block of ice to each side of the
vessel with our kedge-anchor and grapnels. As the blocks of ice
drew nine or ten fathoms of water, I thought that they would save
us if we were driven ashore, as they would run aground before we
did. But the plan didn't work, so I sent the boat—which was now
repaired—to see if she could find a more secure place for our ship.

As soon as she had left the ship, however, she was trapped in the
ice, and the men were forced to haul her up on an ice-floe to prevent
her from being crushed. They dragged her over the ice from one
floe to another, looking for open water. Meanwhile, because of the
movement and grinding of the ice-pack, the two pieces broke away
from our sides, carrying with them our kedge-anchor and grapnels.
We signalled the boat to return to the ship, which she did with great
difficulty, the men being forced to haul her over many pieces of ice.
In the meantime, we set some sail and worked our way to the piece
of ice that was carrying our grapnel, which we recovered. By this
time our boat had caught up with us, and I sent her with a fresh
crew to fetch our kedge-anchor. This they set out to do with great
danger to both boat and men.

By this time the ship had been driven so near the shore that we
could see the rocks under us and all around us. And we were carried
by the whirlings of the waters almost upon the points of rock, but
then mercifully swept back again. As this was happening in spite of
the sail we had set, we expected momentarily that she would be
beaten to pieces. So, in desperation, I set more sail and drove her in
amongst the rocks and grounded icebergs. We passed over rocks
that had but 12 or 13 feet of water over them, and so let go an
anchor.

The anchor, by itself, would never have been able to fetch up the
ship, but by good fortune she was stopped by a great piece of ice
that was aground. In the process, she broke the main knee of her
beak-head,[11] and a jagged piece of ice tore away four of our main
shrouds. Finally, an anchor that we had lashed to our bow caught
in the ice and ground us to a halt. Thus did we come to anchor. We

saw that we were in 15 feet of water, with sharp rocks under us and all around us; we were also in a spot where the tide would drive the ice upon us. Our boat was not to be seen, which led us to fear that she had been crushed to pieces along with the third part of our company. But eventually we saw her come about a point amongst the rocks. She had recovered our kedge-anchor which cheered us up somewhat. With all speed we laid out hawsers to the rocks, and with everyone working manfully, warped her out of that dangerous place and up to the side of the rocks. There we had three fathom of water, and were sheltered by a large grounded iceberg which we hoped would protect us from drifting ice. During the ebb-tide, we lay there very comfortably; but when the flood came, we were assaulted by pieces of ice that put us in great distress. We had to work hard and continuously to ward off the drifting ice. At full flood, the grounded block of ice which had been shielding us suddenly went adrift, leaving us in a most eminent danger. But when the ebb started, our buckler was again grounded in a very favourable place, and sheltered us during the rest of the tide.

All through the night we worked at shifting our cables and hawsers to higher points on the rocks so that drifting ice could pass under them. All day and all night it snowed heavily, while a violent west wind piled a veritable sea of ice upon us. In trying to protect ourselves from the ice, we broke the fluke from our kedge-anchor, and two arms from our grapnels; we parted two hawsers, and seriously damaged the shallop again. I put all hands to work repairing it.

During that tide, the harbour was so choked with ice that it seemed to be a solid, immovable sheet. But with the ebb, it started to break up and move. Then, when some of the larger pieces were grounded they altered the course of the drifting ice and put us on the rocks. In spite of all our efforts, the ship settled against a sharp rock which rose about a yard above our main-mast. And as the water ebbed away, she hung after the head, and heeled to the offing.[12] We fastened cables and hawsers to the masts high above the deck, attached their other ends to the rocks and pulled them taut with tackles. But as the water continued to fall, the vessel heeled over so much that we could not stand up.

Having now done all that we could—but to little purpose—we left the vessel, and knelt in prayer on an ice floe, beseeching God to be merciful unto us. It was still an hour to low water, and the tide would have to drop another foot and a half before it reached the level of the previous tide. We had carefully noted earlier lows, setting up stones and other markers so that we would make no mistake. By this time the ship had heeled over so far that the gunwale in the forecastle was under water, and we expected her to capsize at any minute. Indeed, at one point, the cables parted and she settled down half a foot, but then, unexpectedly, the water began to rise. We could actually see the water rising, and the ship with it. Then was our sorrow turned to joy, and we all fell to our knees, praising God for his mercy in so miraculous a deliverance.

As soon as the ship was freed from the rock, we worked to get her farther off. During the flood we were not too seriously pestered by the ice, but with the ebb it again came driving down upon us, placing us in great extremity. To form a barrier, we put as many pieces as possible between us and the rocks. Suddenly a huge piece of ice loomed on our quarter, a piece more than 300 paces in circumference. Fortunately, it grounded as did several other large floes, so that this tide the harbour was so choked up with ice that a man could walk over it in any direction. When the tide was three quarters of the way out, the large floes that were grounded began to break up with a most terrible, thundering noise. We were afraid that those that were close to us would crush us when they broke apart, but God preserved us.

On the morning of the 22nd, the water dropped two feet lower than the previous tide, thus showing us God's mercies in our late extremity. During that flood we had some respite from our labours, but after full sea, our hopes ebbed too. The large floe that was grounded near us blocked the channel so that all the ice came driving down upon us. We thought for a while that we would lose our ship. But we went to work with axes, iron bars and anything else we could find to knock the sharp corners off the ice-floes, and to keep the channel as open as possible so that the ice could drift past. It pleased God to make our labours successful. Thus we made

way for some pieces, and fended off the rest, and got so much rotten
ice between us and the rocks that we were fairly secure. But at low
tide, the grounded ice-floes that were breaking up around us made a
most thunderous din.

That day I went ashore and built a large stone beacon upon the
highest point of the island. I topped it with a cross and named our
harbour The Harbour of God's Providence. In the evening the
harbour was more solidly packed with ice than at any time since our
arrival, for the larger pieces grounded and stopped the rest from
moving out with the tide. And the ship lay there as in a bed of ice.

On the morning of the 23rd, the ice again drove up amongst the
broken ground with the flood; and with the ebb, it all drifted out (it
being then very calm) except one giant floe which was grounded
not far from us. It settled itself in such a manner that we felt threatened by its presence. But nothing happened, so I took the boat and
went ashore on the eastern side of the harbour to see if I could find
a safer place than our unfortunate harbour. Amongst the rocks, I
saw such a likely place, a small cove. From the top of the hill where
I was standing, I could see the ship. It was almost slack water, when
suddenly the large grounded ice-floe broke into four pieces with
a terrifying noise. As the block of ice rose to half the height of our
mast, I was afraid that it might have damaged our ship. Hurrying to
the boat, I rowed back to the ship where, thank God, I found that
all was well.

I instantly sent the boat to sound the channel leading to the cove I
had seen from the hill-top. This was a very dangerous passage for
the boat. On her return, we cast off, and as swiftly as possible
warped her away from amongst that terrible ice. When we were less
than a mile away, the whole field of ice disintegrated, and would
surely have taken us with it, were it not for God's mercy. We
warped our way about the rocks, and into the little cove that I had
just discovered. There we made fast to the rocks, thinking that we
were probably safe. When this was done, I again went ashore where
I wandered around to see what I could discover. I found it to be
broken, rocky ground with not so much as a tree, an herb or a blade

of grass upon it. Some ponds were noted, but as these had not yet
thawed, there were no water-fowl around. Nor did we see any deer
or bear tracks, but we did see one or two foxes.

We found a place where some natives had camped a long time ago.
They had built fires and we found a few pieces of charred wood
scattered about them, together with some fox bones and whale
bones. I could not figure out why anyone would have camped at
such a place, for there was almost no driftwood along the shore, and
no fish at all. At least we were never able to catch one although we
tried daily. Or, perhaps it was not the right time of year. I named
the cove Price's Cove, after the master of my ship. Its latitude is 61°
north, and the variation of the compass there is 24°. The chips and
pieces of charred wood that I mentioned earlier had been cut with
a hatchet or other instrument of iron.

From the top of the hills, we could see the islands that are on the
south shore, and commonly called Sir Thomas Button's Isles. They
did bear south and by east, half a point easterly, some 14 or 15
leagues distant. Upon the change day, it flows here seven o'clock
and a half, with the highest tide being three fathoms at most.[13] The
flood comes from the eastward and thither it returns.

From the top of the hill, I had been watching the huge pieces of ice
floating two or three leagues from shore. They moved back and
forth indifferently with the flood and ebb of the tide, showing me
that there was no current in those parts. Near the shore, there are
innumerable eddies when the tide is ebbing because of the broken
ground and stranded ice-floes there. In addition, there are numerous
submerged rocks whose depths vary with the state of the tide, and
these uncertainties cause similar distractions. I would therefore
advise no one to go too near those shores for fear of losing his ship,
and with it himself. Our last night in the cove we had more rest than
in the ten previous nights.

The next morning, June 24th, a fair gale sprang up from the east.
So after prayer, we untied our ship and set sail, steering between
great pieces of ice that were stranded in 40 fathom of water, and

rose twice the height of our mast-head. We went forth from this
cove on the flood, and had none of those whirlings of the waters
that we had met with on entering the cove. We tried to reach the
north shore so we stayed within a league of Resolution Island where
we had some ice-free water to sail through. In the offing, however,
the pack was solid, and by twelve o'clock it had us trapped. In spite
of a strong east wind, we could not get through it. Meanwhile, the
sharp corners of the ice grated against us with such violence that I
verily thought it would have grated the planks from the sides of the
ship. Thus we continued to be tormented till the 26th, drifting back
and forth with the ice, and being unable to see even an acre from
the mast-head.

The 26th was a calm, sunny day, and we measured the latitude and
compass variation. We also took soundings and found a bottom of
fine white sand at 140 fathom. I had the men rig some fishing lines,
but to no purpose, for I couldn't see that the bait had even been
touched. The nights were so very cold that our rigging froze, and
pools of fresh water on the surface of the ice were themselves
covered by half an inch of ice.

On the 27th a small gale sprang up from the southeast and broke
up the ice-pack a bit, so we set the foresail and forced the ship forward. In the evening, the wind became contrary, shifting to west
northwest, which forced us to fasten our ship to a huge ice-floe
where we remained moored till the 29th.

On the 28th I determined that there was no current in the strait by
a number of experiments that I carried out. Specifically, I took a
number of bearings on land, and noted over a period of several
days that we simply drifted to and fro with the ebb and flood of
the tide. I checked this in both calm and stormy weather. By all
these experiments, I found that the tide was no stronger there than
it is between England and France.

On the morning of the 29th, there sprang up a fine gale from the
east which broke up the ice enough that we could force our ship
through it with her fore-sail. By twelve o'clock we were in open

water, with the wind holding steady in the east and the weather so
clear that we could see the Island of Resolution. It was about 12
leagues away, with its north end bearing east northeast.

## July, 1631

From the 29th of June to the 5th of July, we sailed through the ice
with variable winds and fogs, and occasional calms. At noon we
had a good observation and found that our latitude was 63° 15′
north. Shortly afterwards, we saw Salisbury Island[14] bearing west
by north some seven leagues away, with much ice in between. This
made us stand to the northward. Next we saw Prince Charles' Cape,
and Mill Island.[15] And all around us—but particularly to the north
northwest—the sea was most infinitely pestered with ice. This did
grieve me very much, for determined as I was to explore to the
northwest, I saw that it was not possible that year. In addition, we
were again driven back by head-winds, were still trapped in the ice
and were exposed to such perils and dangers that we thought on a
thousand occasions that our ship would be smashed to pieces.

By the 15th of July, we were between Digges Island[16] and Nottingham Island,[17] but could not get farther north. And then—for an
hour or two—we actually had some open water.

Before proceeding with my narrative, however, I would like to
describe Hudson Strait which stretches from Resolution Island in
the east, to Digges Island in the west. If you include the coastline of
the large bay on the south side, the strait is about 120 leagues long,
and trends west northwest and east southeast. It is about 15 leagues
wide, except towards the western end where it is somewhat wider.
It is about 20 leagues from Digges Island to Cape Charles between
which lie Salisbury and Nottingham islands. On a clear day, you
can see both the north and the south shores. Generally, the depth in
the middle of the strait is 120 fathom; the bottom is white sand, and
apart from tidal streams, there is no current. The north shore is the
straighter and less encumbered with ice. Along the shore, there are
many low, small islands which cannot be detected from any distance, but make the shoreline look as though it were indented by

innumerable small bays. The mainland, on both sides of the strait, is moderately high. Let this suffice. You may get the details from the chart.

Having decided by the 16th that it was impossible to get through the ice to the north-west, I told the master of my ship to steer west southwest, towards Mansfield's Island.[18] We arrived there at three o'clock the next afternoon, having had very foul weather, and having struck some fearful blows against the ice. That day, too, we cut our allowance of bread in half on meat days, and rationed other supplies as sparingly as we could. Two of the men complained of sickness that day, but soon recovered.

In the evening, after anchoring the vessel, I sent the boat ashore to check the tides. They told me that while they were ashore, the tide rose some three feet. And we found from the swing of the ship on her anchor, as well as from the floating ice, that the tidal current comes from the west southwest. The tide didn't rise above two fathom, so far as we could judge. On Mansfield's Island, fireplaces and heaps of stones showed that the natives had visited there at one time; fox tracks were the only other sign of life. Then the wind turned so contrary, and the weather so foggy, that we had to fire some guns so that the men in the boat could find us.

Next morning—the 17th—the wind became more favourable so we weighed anchor. Although the ice was very thick in the offing, the shore itself was fairly clear, so we followed it some 10 leagues to the south and south by west. In the afternoon, the wind shifted against us, so we anchored again about a mile from shore. Farther out, the sea was thick with ice, and completely impassable. This time I went myself to check up on the tide, and found that while I was ashore it flowed two feet and that the tidal current came from the southwest by west. I saw signs that the natives had been on the island; but there was almost no driftwood on the shore, nor were there animals on the land nor fish in the sea. We saw some birds, killed one and then returned to the ship. Mansfield's Island is very low, little higher than a sand-bank. It has a few fresh-water ponds, but no grass. It is utterly barren.

On the morning of July 18th the wind became more favourable, so
we weighed anchor and set sail, for we were being surrounded by
ice. We tried to sail due west, intending to make a land-fall at about
63°north. By twelve o'clock we came to a solid wall of pack ice, but
it pleased God to increase the wind, and we sailed away to the
south southwest, in latitude 62° north. By four in the afternoon, we
were in open water and joyfully steered away to the west, and west
by north. But our high spirits didn't last long. By 10 o'clock that
night we heard the growling of the ice, and at the same time we were
wrapped in a thick, black fog. Nevertheless we stayed on course,
and the closer we came to the ice, the more hideous did the noise
become.

On the 19th, about three in the morning, we reached it, and as the
fog lifted a little, we could see slabs of ice as thick as any we had
yet seen. As there was no way through the ice, and as the wind was
in the northwest, we coasted along it, hoping to get around it to the
south. Finally, however, we became so blinded by fog, and so
jammed in the ice that we could go no further. In spite of the fog,
we tried to beat to the westward the next morning—the 20th—with
our ship pounding against the ice most fearfully. We continued
stubbornly on course till the 21st, when we were again trapped by
the ice in latitude 60° 33′ north.

While we were trapped there, I inspected the ship to see what damage she might have suffered from the beating she had taken. We
noticed that she was all bruised and broken below the iron plate
that protected her cut-water; the two knee-braces which strength-
ened her bow were torn and twisted; and there were many other
defects which we had no way of correcting. In spite of the damage
and an extremely thick fog, we continued our hazardous journey
till the 27th, even though we could not see the distance of a pistol-
shot in any direction.

The weather finally cleared when the wind shifted to the south,
dispersing the ice, and allowing us to continue to the west. In the
evening, we were again trapped in the ice with the wind veering
from the south to the east, and blowing a fresh gale. It was particu-

larly upsetting that we could make no progress with such a favourable wind. So we fastened our ship to a large ice-floe, and patiently
waited till our fortunes should improve. Since leaving Mansfield
Island, our soundings had varied between 100 and 110 fathom with
a mud bottom. Now, suddenly, the water began to shoal. On the
27th, drifting with the pack, we measured but 80 fathom.

Through the 28th and 29th, we were trapped solidly in the ice.
When we spread all our sails to a very heavy gale, the ship moved
no more than if she had been in dry-dock! Leaving the vessel with
all sails set, we went out on the ice for some sport and recreation.
The ice there was in large flat cakes—up to 1,000 paces long—and
the most difficult to deal with that we had so far encountered.

That was the day the men started to grumble, thinking that it was
impossible for us to move either forward or backward. Some believed that there was solid pack-ice between us and the western
shore. Others believed that the entire bay was covered with ice, and
they doubted that we would be able to move in any direction, or
find any land to winter in. The nights were long, and every night it
froze so hard that we could not move through the ice. Nor could
we sail any more in thick, foggy weather. I comforted and encouraged the men as best I could. To divert them, we drank a toast to
His Majesty on the ice; we left not one man on the ship which just
stood there locked in the ice with all sails set. I must honestly confess that the grumbling of the men was not without reason. I, too,
suspected that we might be frozen in the ice all winter. I therefore
ordered that a fire should be lighted only once a day; that only so
many pieces of wood were to be used for each fire; and that the
steward should deliver these to the cook by actual count. These
measures were designed to make our fuel last as long as possible.

On the 30th, we moved the ship forward by heaving it with our
shoulders, breaking up the ice with mauls and crow-bars to clear a
path. As we moved forward, the water shoaled rapidly, which led
me to believe that we were near some island. At noon, we checked
our latitude through patches of fog by using the quadrant on an ice-
floe. Our position was 58° 4′ north; our depth was 30 fathom. We

put out hooks to try to catch some fish, but to no purpose, for there
are none in that bay. On the 31st, we continued breaking up the ice
and pushing the ship forward. At noon our latitude was 58° 40′, the
depth of water was 23 fathom. There was a thick haze that day, or
else I think we should have seen the land.

**August, 1631**

The first day of August, a west wind drove us eastwards where our
depth increased to 35 fathom. At noon, an observation with the
quadrant on the ice showed us that our latitude was 58° 45′ north.
At six o'clock that night, we could feel the ice rising and falling a
little because of a slight swell that came out of the southwest. This
was a great comfort to us, as it raised the hope that we might shortly
be freed from the ice. But on the second, in spite of a strong southwest wind, we could no longer feel the swell which we hoped would
break up the pack.

Two days later we could see a little open water to the northwest,
and could feel a gentle swell rolling in from the west, suggesting
open water ahead. By the 5th, we could actually see the open water,
but were unable to reach it with our sails. So we anchored in 50
fathoms of water about six in the evening, and spent the entire night
using poles and oars to fend off the ice, and let it drift to leeward.

On the morning of August 6th, we weighed anchor, and with a
northwest wind and great joy we headed for the open sea to the
south. By noon we were successful, being totally free of ice in latitude 58° 28′ north. Suddenly the wind shifted to a more favourable
quarter, so we stood away to the northwest, hoping to reach the
shore at the highest possible northern latitude, and then follow the
coastline south. Then we knelt in prayer, thanking God for deliver-
ing us out of the ice. On the 9th, at 59° 40′ north, we again
encountered ice, and noted that it was very thick to the north. Since
we came out of the ice, the depth had increased to 110 fathom; but
as it was now shoaling, I though that we were approaching land.
The next day the weather being thick and foggy with a contrary
wind, and the water shoaling rapidly, we anchored in 22 fathom.

We weighed anchor on the morning of the 11th and headed for
shore, making land-fall about noon at 59° 40′ north when we were
in 16 fathom of water. To the north of us, the land trended north
by east; to the south, around a point, it trended west by south. We
followed that shore, heading for a place that was formerly called
Hubbert's Hope.[19] And so indeed it had been, but now it was
hopeless.

Let us now pause for a moment to say a few words regarding the
bay we have just crossed over. From Digges Island to the western
shore at 59° 40′ north is about 160 leagues, the course being west
southwest.[20] Although tidal current is shaped by the contours of
the land in shoal water, in the middle of the bay it runs east and
west, as we observed on many occasions. But in the ocean or in
large bays, I believe that the tidal current naturally sets east and
west. This gives little hope for a northwest passage, as it suggests
that we are probably in an enclosed bay. The greatest depth of
water we found in the bay was 110 fathom, with gradual shoaling
as land was approached.

But back to the voyage. We coasted around Hubbert's Hope and
found it to be a little bay some 18 leagues deep. It shoaled from
six or eight fathom to two and a half fathom of water at the bottom
of the bay where we were almost completely surrounded by land.
We then proceeded southward in six or seven fathom of water,
staying within sight of the land, taking continuous soundings and
anchoring at night. We anchored last night—the 11th—with our
kedge-anchor as there was very little wind, and in the morning we
lost it, the last one we had. On the 12th we were at 58° 46′ north,
about two leagues from shore, where the variation was 17°.

During the afternoon of the 13th, a somewhat hazy day, we suddenly saw breakers ahead. We were in nine or ten fathom of water
then and had swung the vessel up into the wind to clear the reef
when we suddenly struck the rocks.[21] We were carrying both top-
sails, the fore-sail and sprit-sail at the time, and were pushed along
by a fresh gale of wind. In this fearful position we frantically struck
all our sails. Then it pleased God to send two or three good swelling

seas which heaved us over the rocks and into three fathom, then
three and a half fathom, where we dropped the anchor. We manned
the pumps, and found the ship had not taken in any water in spite
of her terrible pounding. We had thought that her mast would be
reduced to splinters, and that her bilges would surely have been
stove in.

We hoisted the boat overboard, double-manned her and sent her off
to find us a way out of that perilous place. They were no sooner
gone than a fog rolled in, and we had to fire some guns so that they
would know where we were. Fortunately the wind dropped, otherwise it is doubtful whether they would ever have been able to get
back to the ship. After an absence of about two hours, the men
brought us word that there were rocks and shoals all around us, but
that they had found a channel with at least two and a half fathom
of water that would lead us out of our peril. So we weighed anchor
and followed the boat, crossing two ledges over which there was
scarcely 14 feet of water. Then the depth gradually dropped off to 3,
4, and finally 14 fathom, but shoaled again to 9. As it was late in
the afternoon by this time, we anchored there, and rode out the
night fairly well.

In the morning contrary winds kept us at anchor, so I decided to
tidy up the ship, to make sure the holds were in order and to splice
any cables that needed it. We also looked to our anchors, and fitted
out some spare ones. Finally, we got the bruised and battered long-
boat from between the decks and set the carpenter to fixing her. For
I intended to tow the shallop, and keep the long-boat on deck, so
that both should be ready at a moment's notice to lay out anchors,
or to perform any service with which God might be pleased to try
our faith and patience. For in Him was our only trust, and our
honest endeavours could only hope for success through His favour.

At noon, when our latitude was 57° 45′, we could see land from
the northwest to the southeast by east, as well as many rocks and
shoals. The rocks that we passed over in the channel were now
above water, so I know that the tide there was at least two fathom.
At noon I sent the boat to take soundings to the eastward because

the water had been shoaling rapidly when we reached our anchorage. She reported the shoalest water to be seven fathom. We
intended to weigh anchor immediately, but the wind suddenly
shifted to the east so that we could not budge, but lay there all
night in a stiff gale.

During the evening of the 15th, our anchor cable became so frayed
that it parted. Because this perilous and sudden accident left us no
time to attach a buoy to the cable, we lost the anchor, and were
driven into four fathom of water before we could set our sails. When
they were set, we steered south southeast with an east wind until
the water shoaled to three fathom. Then we swung around to north
northeast, and the water gradually deepened to 10 fathom, where
we anchored for the night because it was beginning to grow dark.
On the morning of the 16th, a fresh gale was blowing from the north
so we raised the anchor and got under weigh. By nine o'clock, it
developed into a very storm so we drifted back and forth all day in
10 fathom. When the wind dropped in the evening, we sailed southwest towards Port Nelson steering all night by the stars. We were at
57° 25' north, where the variation was about 17°.

We stood south the next morning, with the bottom dropping off
gradually to eight fathoms. At noon we had a reliable sight, and
calculated our latitude to be 57° 15', which would put us within
six or seven leagues of the southern side of Port Nelson. At that
place the colour of the water changed to a puddlish, sandy-red. We
stood into six fathom, but could still not see any land from the
top-mast head. So, as night was falling, and the wind was beginning
to freshen from east by south, we stood off again into 10 or 12
fathom where the water was again the colour of the sea.

As the storm had blown itself out by the 18th, and both wind and
weather were favourable, we stood again to the south. Then, as we
once more entered the puddlish water, it shoaled to six or eight
fathom, at which point a thick fog forced us to stand off again. All
day and all night the lead was used constantly. The 19th was a fine
and sunny day, so we stood again into the thick puddlish water and
anchored in eight fathom so we could measure the tide. No land

was visible, but at noon we checked our latitude and found that we
were at 57° 27′ north, with the tide setting northwest by west and
southeast by east. I decided that there was nothing but shoals
between us and the shore.

In the afternoon it began to snuffle and blow so that we had much
trouble raising the anchor. But finally we stood east southeast with
the water shoaling rapidly, but when we changed course to east, it
deepened a little. In the evening, the wind shifted to the west and
we returned to our previous course—east southeast—into ten, then
eight fathom. Thus did we follow our lead and the colour of the
water into six fathom.

On the 20th, at six in the morning, we sighted land, a very low flat
land. To examine it more closely, we stood into five fathom then
stood along it till noon, when we were in latitude 57° north. We
named this land The New Principality of South Wales, and with
our finest liquor we drank a health to His Highness, Prince Charles,
whom God preserve. Standing along the coast we came to a point
where it trended southward, and where there were two small islands.
In the evening it was calm when we anchored, with the tide setting
southeast by east. Because of contrary winds we spent all that night
and the next day there, riding at anchor. There was a short, choppy
sea which laboured the ship rather heavily, driving her sprit-sail
yard and even her forecastle into the swells, for we had not yet
trimmed her properly to ride such seas.

About nine that night, when it was very dark and blowing hard,
soundings showed that we were adrift. When we started to winch in
the cable, thinking that our anchor was already lost, the anchor
suddenly caught, and threw the men from the winch. In the dark, a
small rope had got foul of both the cable and the master's leg, but
with the help of God he freed himself, suffering only some nasty
bruises. Both of our mates were hurt, one in the head, the other in
the arm. One of our strongest men was struck in the chest with a
capstan-bar and lay sprawled on the deck, gasping for breath.
Another had his head in the cable and barely escaped. Many more
were flung about and rather sorely bruised. But our gunner, an

honest and diligent man, had his leg caught between the capstan
and the cable which wrung off his foot, tore all the flesh from his
leg, crushed the bone, and battered his entire body. He lay on the
deck in this miserable condition till we had recovered from our
shock. While we were carrying the gunner and the others down to
the surgeon, the ship drifted into shoal water. We found this terrifying, as we were severely weakened by the tragedy that had just put
eight of our men out of action.

But it pleased God that the anchor should catch once more, and
thus we rode out the night. By midnight the surgeon had taken off
the gunner's leg just below the knee, and had bandaged the others
that were hurt and bruised. After this experience, we comforted
each other as well as we could.

We got under weigh on the 22nd and stood off into deeper water,
expecting a better wind there. In the afternoon, when we were
favoured by the hoped-for wind, we stood in again to the shore and
proceeded to follow it. The water was very shoal and full of reefs
for about four leagues offshore. By the 23rd, at noon, we were in
latitude 56° 28′ north; by evening, the wind was against us, forcing
us to spend the night standing off and on. All that month the wind
had been very variable, never blowing long from the same direction,
and making it impossible for us to continue long on one course.

On the 26th there was a fine west wind, with very poor visibility as
we stood into seven then six fathom of thick, puddlish water. When
it cleared at noon, we saw that we were in a small bay, almost
surrounded by land. We got out of the bay and continued following
the coast till the morning of the 27th, when we encountered higher
land than any we had seen since we left Nottingham Island. We
stood into it and came to anchor in five fathom.

I sent off the boat, well-manned and armed, with instructions in
writing and orders to return to the ship before sunset. The evening
came, but no boat. We fired some guns and made some false fires,[22]
but received no answer, which we found very disturbing. We
suspected that the men had met with some disaster through

43

carelessness. And we knew that if the men in the boat were lost, we
were all lost, for there were not enough men left on board either to
raise the anchor or man the ship. Presently, however, when we saw
a fire upon the shore we were even more upset, for they had
answered neither our musket-shots nor our false fires, with a corres-
ponding signal. We thought, therefore, that the savages had mass-
acred our men, and that it was the fire of the savages that we now
saw on shore. But finally they arrived, all safe and sound, explaining
that as soon as they were ashore the tide went out very suddenly,
leaving them stranded behind a bar of perfectly dry sand. Having
no choice, they waited for the next high tide. With this explanation
I was pacified.

They reported that there was a great quantity of driftwood on the
shore, and that the land itself was thickly wooded. Deer and bear
tracks were seen, and birds were so plentiful that several were shot,
but there was no sign of people. They said that they had crossed two
small streams, and had been stopped by a third.

At low tide we were anchored in only three fathom of water. Therefore, when the wind started blowing rather strongly from the east,
we weighed anchor and stood to the northward till midnight, then
stood in again to shore. In the morning, when we were in sight of
land, the wind again increased, and we were again forced to stand
out to sea, while the wind increased to gale force. Soon we could
not carry even a pair of courses, so we reduced sail to the main
course alone, continuing that way for a day and a night.

By the morning of the 29th, we reckoned that we had been driven
back some 16 or 18 leagues. And then as it cleared, we saw a ship
about three or four leagues to leeward. I sailed up to where she was
anchored in 13 fathom and learned that it was one of His Majesty's
ships under the command of Captain Fox. When I saluted him
according to nautical custom, he returned the salute, so I stood in
toward the shore, thinking I would tack about, get on his weather
side and send over a boat. But a shift in the wind made this impossible. It wasn't till that night that I finally got on his weather side
and sent over a boat. We then stood off and on together for the rest
of the night.

In the morning Captain Fox and his friends came aboard the *Henrietta Maria*; there I entertained them as well as I could under the circumstances and shared with them the fresh meat from the birds my men had shot when they were ashore. I told Captain Fox that I had named this land The South Principality of Wales;[23] I showed him how far I had been to the eastward, and where I had landed; and I warned him of the dangers of all the coast that I had visited. He told me that he, himself, had been in Port Nelson, and before that had carried out only superficial explorations. He had not yet been ashore in the bay, and, in fact, had rarely seen the land. That evening, after I had given his men some tobacco and other things they were short of, Captain Fox returned to his ship. In the morning he stood away to the south southwest, and I never saw him again. And as the wind was favourable to me also, I stood into the shore and continued following it to the east.

The month of August ended with snow and hail, and with the temperature as low as I have ever seen it in England.

**September, 1631**

We followed the 10-fathom line on September 1st till the weather cleared, then we just followed the coast. Presently the water shoaled to five fathom and we saw reefs to leeward, so we swung around to north northeast but still raised land. By nightfall we were out of that dangerous bay, but only with difficulty; and as the wind shifted around to the south at midnight we furled our sails and let the ship drift northward into deeper water. That day, for the first time, the surgeon told me that several of the men were tainted with sickness. At noon our latitude was 55° 12′ north.

On the 2nd, as we stood in again for shore, the weather became winterly and foul just as we were getting into shoal water. The threatened storm struck us as we were again standing off into deeper water. By midnight the storm had blown itself out, so the next morning, the 3rd, we stood in again and raised land by eleven o'clock. There it trended south southeast and south so we knew that we were at a cape. And we named it Cape Henrietta Maria, after

Her Majesty who had given her name also to our ship. At noon we were in latitude 55° 05′ north, which is the latitude of the cape.

From Port Nelson to Cape Henrietta Maria the coast trends generally east southeast, although a number of points and bays will alter this at specific localities as much as two or three points. The distance is about 130 leagues: the variation at the cape, taken by amplitude,[24] is about 16°. This is a shoal and perilous coast, with not a harbour to be found.

During the afternoon of the 3rd, a vicious storm came out of the north and continued till midnight with extreme violence. The next morning, after the storm had blown itself out, we again stood to the southwest. Because the weather was very thick, we had to take soundings continually, but by noon it had cleared up sufficiently for us to see the shore. It trended south by east, with the tidal flow setting along it smartly. In the evening, there came a great rolling sea out of the north northeast and, by eight o'clock, a heavy wind out of the southeast. The conflict of the heavy rolling sea from the northeast and the strong wind from the southeast churned up the surface of the water most frightfully. And to add to the peril of our position, the lightning flashed, the wind roared and it rained and snowed all night. Never before was I in such a storm. We shipped many seas, but one which swept us fore and aft was particularly dangerous. It shook us with such violence that I thought it would surely sink the ship. In this wild distraction of wind and waves, the ship laboured terribly, and we had great difficulty in keeping things lashed down in the hold and between the decks.

The next morning, the 5th, the wind shifted to the southwest but did not alter its disposition—it continued in its old anger and fury. In the afternoon it shifted again to the northwest and there showed its supreme malice. Neither I nor any of the men with me had ever seen the sea lashed to such fury. Our ship was so tormented and belaboured by seas washing over it from both sides and both ends that we were in most miserable distress in this unknown and lonely place. At eight o'clock that night the storm broke up, and we finally had some much-needed rest, as no one had had a wink of sleep

during the last 30 hours. If this storm had continued blowing from
the east where it started, we would all have perished were it not
for God's mercy.

Because a southwest wind prevented us from moving to the westward on the 6th, we spent the day trimming our ship. We carried
aft all of our coal and several other heavy items in order to lighten
the bow. We also sorted out our bread, because much of it was wet.
For no matter what we did, we shipped vast quantities of water
between decks and much of this flowed into the hold, and then into
the bread-room. The sea rolled over us so continually, that we were
like Jonas in the belly of the whale. We also looked to our tacks
and sheets and other rigging because for the future we could expect
nothing but winter weather. That evening, our boatswain, an
industrious man who had laboured mightily the past three or four
days, was very sick. When he fainted two or three times, we felt sure
he was dying.

On the morning of the 7th, before a southeast wind, we stood away
to the southwest with all sails set. Presently we saw an island, and
came close aboard it in 20 fathoms of water. That was the first place
where we had found that depth of water closer than four or five
leagues from shore. The island stands at 54° 10′ north about 14
leagues from the mainland.[25] In the afternoon we stood away to the
southwest, and as we approached the western shore the water
shoaled to seven fathom, but the weather was so thick that we
could still not see the land.

September 8th was thick, foggy and calm, and the weather stayed
that way till about six o'clock the next morning. Although the fog
continued, a wind then came up at south southwest, and we stood to
the eastward on soundings. In the evening the water shoaled to
nine fathoms, so we stood off and on all night. We sighted land on
the 10th, an island some eight or nine leagues long, at 53° 5′ north
and about 15 leagues from the western mainland. The part that we
coasted trends west northwest. I named it My Lord Weston's
Island.[26] Then we continued to the eastward in broken, foggy

weather. In the afternoon, we noticed land to the eastward of
us which seemed to consist of three hills or hummocks. Very cir-
cumspectly we sailed towards them, keeping a constant check on
the depth of water with our lead. Presently we also saw land to the
south of us, so we nosed the vessel up closer to the wind and
headed for it under our main course only, as we had started in a
thick, dark fog. Soon we were in the midst of such broken ground,
rocks and surf that we didn't know which way to turn. Thank God
there was but little wind, so we anchored our ship.

When it cleared soon afterwards, we could see nothing around us
but sands, rocks and shoals, except for the channel we came in. I
therefore sent the boat to take soundings among the shoals and
rocks so that if, in an emergency, we were forced to move, we would
have some idea as to which way to go. Fortunately, the night was
calm and the weather fair, so we rode quietly at anchor. The next
morning I had the boat put me ashore, then continue sounding the
rocks and shoals around us. I found the island to be utterly barren.
I had thought it would be easy to find scurvy-grass, sorrel or some
herb to cure the sick members of my crew, but there was nothing.

I could see that the tide did not ordinarily rise above two feet at the
island. There was much driftwood along the shore, and some of it
had been driven up very high on the north side of the island. From
that I judged that the heaviest winter storms come from the north.

When I returned aboard, I sent a number of the sick men to another
part of the island to see if they themselves could find anything that
might ease their sufferings. At noon, by a reliable observation, our
latitude was 52° 45′ north. In the evening our men returned dejected, so we weighed anchor and stood to the westward, anchoring
in the lee of another island in 20 fathoms.

On the morning of the 12th, a strong wind sprang up from the
southeast, and the ship began to drag her anchor along the soft,
muddy bottom. So we heaved it aboard and set two courses. While
most of the crew were busily setting the top-sails, others who should
have been taking care of the ship, ran her on the rocks through

sheer carelessness. They should have posted proper lookouts and kept a constant check on the depth of water with the sounding lead. The island had been there all night, and even at the last minute they might still have seen it had they not been blinded by conceit and envious rivalry.

The first blow jolted me out of a deep sleep. As I ran out of my cabin and saw the danger we were in, I thought that I was the only one who had been awakened. I thought I would have to prepare myself for entering the next world without any assistance. After I had my feelings somewhat under control, I had to contend with some very poor advice that was offered. Instead of following the suggestion that I should wreak revenge upon those who had brought us into that perilous position, I resolved to get us off those rocks and shoals. First we hauled all of our sails aback, but this didn't help. In fact, it only made us pound more viciously, so we struck and furled all our sails.

We then punched a hole through our stern so that we could run a cable through the cabin to the capstan and then laid out an anchor to heave her astern. All of the casks of water in the hold I had stove in, and manned the pumps to pump it out, intending to do the same with the beer; then I had all our coal thrown overboard. Finally, when all was ready, we dropped an anchor astern from the long-boat. During this whole process, the ship was pounding so fearfully that we saw some of our own planking drift by us. Then, standing to the capstan, we heaved with such a will that the cable broke, and we lost our anchor. Quickly we put out another.

At that point, we couldn't actually tell whether the ship was leaking or not, as we were still pumping out the water from the casks we had stove in, but we were quite certain that she was sinking. We therefore loaded the long-boat with the carpenter's tools, a barrel of bread, a barrel of powder, six muskets, some match,[27] a tinder-box, fish hooks and lines, pitch and oakum and whatever else we could think of. All this we sent ashore so that we might prolong our miserable lives for a few more days. For five hours the ship continued to pound on the rocks. We were sure that each blow was the last that she could possibly endure. During this pounding, we could not see any change in the level of the tide, but at length it pleased God that we be driven over the shoals and into deeper water.

As we didn't know how our ship was holding together, I put all hands to the pumps till she was empty: only then could we tell how fast she was taking on water. We found her to be leaking badly, but still we knelt in prayer and gave thanks to God that it was no worse. So we brought our gear and supplies back aboard, moved further off the reefs and dropped our anchor.

In the evening, it began to blow very hard from the west southwest. Had it done this while we were on the reef, we would have lost our ship beyond redemption. Again we were forced to weigh anchor and let her drift into the broken ground and rocks to the eastward, with the long-boat sounding out the channel ahead of us. Finally, when we were surrounded by surf, the boat signalled us that we could go no farther. Again we anchored amongst the rocks, where we rode out the night, and where the exhausted crew got what rest it could. That was the place where I first noticed there was almost no tide when there was a south wind. This meant that we were unable to careen the ship to examine her bilges for damage. All we could do was pump.

At noon on September 13th we weighed anchor and stood to the westward where the number of shoals and sunken rocks made us marvel that we had ever got through them in a thick fog. Then, after swinging to the northward and consulting my associates, I decided to beat my way around this island and its surrounding shoals, and go to the bottom of Hudson Bay to see if I could find a way into the River of Canada.[28] And if that failed, then I would winter on the mainland where we could expect to be more comfortable than among these rocks and islands. So we stood along the shore in sight of many reefs and shoals; at dusk, we furled everything but the fore-sail, pushing ahead slowly, and taking constant soundings. Finally, the water shoaled to 10 fathom, and the wind increased sharply so we tacked about and the water deepened to 12

to 14 fathom. When it finally shoaled again to eight fathom, we
tacked about, but it continued to shoal; at five fathom we struck our
sail and dropped anchor, knowing that our resolution to ride out
the storm was a matter of life or death. All through the night, we
rode at anchor in such turbulence that we thought the cable would
tear the bits right out of the vessel.

At daybreak on the 14th, we were very happy men. When we
looked about us, we spotted an island bearing west by north about
two leagues off. What we were in was the shoal water surrounding
that island. As a rather swift tidal current was running—in several
different directions at once, it seemed—we used it to advantage:
we weighed anchor and stood to the northwest to get clear of the
shoal. A northeast wind came up in the afternoon, so we stood
along the eastern shore of the island, in sight of a multitude of
reefs. In the evening a storm hit us, churning up a very heavy sea
which swamped our shallop. We had been towing it astern with
two hawsers when it filled with water. Though still afloat, half the
time it floated upside down, spinning around at the end of its moorings. This made our ship yaw very badly so that seas washed over
us continually. Still we persisted, for we hoped to recover her.

All night the high wind assaulted us, and in the morning rain and
very thick weather were added to our miseries. Suddenly the water
began to shoal so rapidly, and the water became so rough, that we
had to take in our last shred of canvas. And what was equally
serious, there was no possibility that an anchor would hold in such
a situation. All we could do was to prepare ourselves for death,
to meet with dignity the final hours of a miserable and tormented
life. About noon, when visibility improved, we saw two islands
under our lee. We headed in that direction, hoping to find shelter
between them while it was still daylight. For we knew that we were
surely lost if we stayed out at sea that night. Finally we met with
success, dropping our anchor in a protected sound. There we rode
out the night in safety, slowly recovering from the weariness that
resulted from continual labour.

On our way into that harbour, we lost our shallop when the hawsers

parted. This was serious as we now had only the long-boat and she
was terribly bruised and battered. The island that sheltered us was
the one that we had named Lord Weston's Island, when we coasted
along its western shore a few days before. We remained there till
the 19th, with the wind so high and the snow so thick that we didn't
dare to launch our long-boat, which the carpenter worked on
almost constantly.

The 19th, when the wind shifted to the north northeast, we weighed
anchor and stood to the south. But by noon the wind had shifted
to the south, forcing us to anchor under the lee of another island
which we named The Earl of Bristol's Island.[29] I went ashore, and
wandered around without seeing any signs of natives; nor could I
find any fish, fowl or herbs upon it, so I returned disconsolate to
my ship. With the wind in the north, the tide rose almost six feet,
with the flood setting to the south. High tide, that day, was at one
o'clock.

A strong north wind prevented us from getting around the island,
and thus to the south, so we discussed what we should do about
finding a wintering place. Some of the men advised me to go back
to Port Nelson where we knew there was a cove in which the ship
might winter safely. I didn't like that suggestion because Port Nelson
is a perilous place, and it would take us so long to get there that
we might be caught in the ice. In addition, the higher northern latitude of Port Nelson would probably mean that the weather there
would be worse. And even at our present latitude it was so cold
that our rigging froze every night, and many mornings we had to
shovel six inches of snow off our decks. I decided, therefore, to stand
again to the south, and there to look for some little creek or cove
where we could winter our ship.

We weighed anchor in a thick fog on September 21st, and with a
north wind we stood away to the southwest to clear the shoals that
were on the point of the island, at 53° 10′ north latitude. When we
were clear, we stood to the south. At noon the fog turned into rain
with very thick weather: all afternoon it thundered and looked as
though a storm would hit us at any minute, but we continued on

our course. When the wind increased in the evening, we furled all
our sails and let the ship drift to the south under bare poles, heaving
the lead every half hour. The depth, when we furled our sails, was
30 fathom but gradually increased to 45 fathom, which was a great
comfort to us in the dark.

Suddenly, at midnight, the water began to shoal; as fast as we could
heave the lead the depth dropped to 20 fathom, so we dropped the
anchor and trimmed the ship aft to ride out the storm. There was no
need to warn the men to keep a sharp watch; for not one of them
put his eyelids together all that night. And so we rode it out in spite
of a heavy sea and a very high wind.

When we looked about us the next morning, the 22nd, we saw an
island under our lee. It was a few leagues off, and separated from
us by a tangle of reefs and shoals. We attempted to heave up our
anchor at noon, with the help of the windward tide, although the sea
was still running very high. Pooling all of our strength and experience, we raised it—thanks be to God. But before we could set our
sails, we were driven into nine fathom. When we tried to double
around a point to get under the lee of the island, the water shoaled
to five fathom. Once we were around the point, however, it gradually deepened, and we stood into a fine anchorage. And it was just
in time, for the wind increased to a very gale. Thus we rode out
the storm in reasonable comfort, and recovered somewhat from
our weariness.

All through the night and into the next day it was very cold, with
snow and hail. Nevertheless, I took the boat and went ashore to
look for some creek or cove where we might winter our ship. For
she was very leaky, and the men had become sickly and weak
because of so much pumping and extreme labour. When we reached
the shore, there was nothing but ledges of rock and banks of sand
with a very heavy surf breaking upon them. However, I made the
men row through it and deposit three of us on the island. I then
sent the boat outside of the surf, with orders to wait for me at
anchor. Next, I headed for the top of a hill to see if I could find a
safe wintering place. There was none in sight.

At this point there was a sharp increase in the wind, so we hurried back to the shore. There we found that the tide had ebbed so low that the boat could not get near us, and we were forced to wade out through the surf. The men were so chilled as a result of that drenching they will probably complain of it to their dying days. But then it began to blow so hard that we could not get up-wind to the ship. Nor could we return to the island because of the surf. All we could do was to keep rowing for our lives. Meanwhile, the men on the ship floated a buoy downwind to us on a long warp. With God's assistance it reached us, and we were hauled aboard the vessel where we all rejoiced together.

To us this was a premonition. From now on we would have to be more careful in sending off the boat, for winter was already upon us. I named the island Sir Thomas Roe's Island. Located at 52° 10′ north, it is covered with small trees, but has little else to recommend it. At noon we headed for another island some four leagues to the south southeast which was the highest land we had yet seen in the bay. But as we approached it, the water suddenly shoaled to four fathom so we quickly struck our sails and dropped the anchor. As the bottom was very foul, we had but three fathom under her stern when the anchor finally held. When the weather cleared, we could see a line of breakers under our lee. Because we could not safely remain there, we raised the anchor, moved out into deep water and stood over again for Sir Thomas Roe's Island. By nightfall we were some two leagues downwind of the island and well sheltered.

The tides rise and fall very quickly there among the shoals, and the times of high and low tide are very uncertain. The tidal currents, too, are so very uncertain that it is impossible to sail by compass. Each night therefore, we were forced to seek a new refuge where we could drop our anchor.

On the morning of the 24th, we were threatened by low, sullen clouds and an approaching storm, so we took advantage of the windward tide to get closer under the island. The weather was very thick and foggy, and as we stood to the northeastward, the depth

of water became very irregular. At one cast of the lead we had
twenty fathom, the next seven, then ten, five, eight and three. A
quick swing to the other tack, and things only got worse, the
currents confounding our best judgements in the thick fog where
we had no landmarks to guide us. But it pleased God that we got
clear of the shoals and reefs, although we were not permitted to
gain the lee of the island. So we came to anchor in 35 fathom some
two leagues from shore. All that afternoon we had snow and hail—
and indeed all night as well—and were painful cold.

We weighed anchor on the 25th, hoping to get to the eastward; but
as we tacked back and forth, the wind shifted into our very teeth
and drove us to within a quarter of a mile of shore. There we
dropped the anchor and rode out the storm for life or death.
Amongst all those shoals and broken ground, we endured similar
miseries day after day. Actually, we were even more desperate
than I have related (although the reading of our desperation, perchance, is very unpleasant), what with snow, hail and storms, and
colder weather than I had ever seen in England. Two or three times
each day we had to drop our sheet-anchor; and the extreme labour
of raising it over and over again simply added to our misery.

We thought that all this, which lasted till the 30th of September,
would surely have put an end to our miseries. For we were driven
amongst rocks, shoals, reefs and surfs till we knew not which way
to turn, and were forced to anchor amongst them in an extremity
of peril. And all those perils made a most hideous and terrible noise
in the night. Therefore, I hope it will not be accounted ridiculous
if I tell you of some meditations which occurred to me, now and
then, amidst my ordinary prayers. I offer them to the reader in these
few ragged and torn rhymes:

Oh, my poor soul, why doest thou grieve to see,
So many deaths mustered to murder me?
Look to thyself, regard not me; for I
Must do, (for what I came), perform, or die.
So thou must free thy self from being in
A dung-hill dungeon; a mere sink of sin,
And happily be freed, if thou believe,

Truly in God through Christ, and ever live.
Be therefore glad yet: ere thou go from hence,
For our joint sins, lets do some penitence,
Unfeignedly together. When we part,
I'll with the angels joy, with all my heart.
We have with confidence relied upon
A rusty wire, touched with a little stone,
Incompast round with paper, and alas
To house it harmless, nothing but a glass,
And thought to shun a thousand dangers, by
The blind direction of this senseless fly.
When the fierce winds shatter'd black nights asunder,
Whose pitchy clouds, spitting forth fire and thunder,
Hath shook the earth, and made the ocean roar,
And run to hide it in the broken shore,
Now thou must steer by faith; a better guide
T'will bring thee safe to heaven against the tide
Of Satan's malice. Now let quiet gales
Of saving Grace, inspire thy zealous sails.

## October, 1631

As the 1st of October was a fairly clear day, we sent out our boat
on a windward tide to sound out a channel that might lead us out
of that perilous place. Within two hours, the boat returned with the
news that a channel had been found where there was not less than
12 fathom. When we stood into the channel, however, we found a
totally different situation; we found ourselves among strange currents and reefs together with a heavy, breaking sea. As we proceeded, the water shoaled to six fathom. But we had no choice. We
had to keep going because it was not safe to anchor, and any
direction in which we might hope to turn offered us nothing but
certain death. But it pleased God to lead us through.

The water sometimes deepened to 20 fathom, then, suddenly,
shoaled to five fathom. So we dropped the anchor, struck all of our
sails and rode out the gale till midnight, lashed by a merciless wind
and a heavy and turbulent sea. And as the bottom was very poor
holding-ground, we thought every minute that our anchor would

 drag.

The next morning—the 2nd—was very calm, so I sent out the boat on a favourable tide to take soundings. Two hours later they returned, reporting that they had located a safe anchorage. When we raised our anchor, we found that the cable had been frayed in two places and would soon have parted if the foul weather had continued. We attempted to follow the boat, but since there was not enough wind we dropped the anchor in 18 fathom. I then took the boat, and went south to an island which I named after the Earl of Danby.[30]

From the highest point on the island. I could see nothing but shoals and reefs to the south. It looked even worse than anything we had already been through. I noted that the island had been visited by the natives and that it was heavily wooded. Hurrying to the boat, I took soundings in the bay, for fear of shoals and sunken rocks, and found it fairly clear. Late in the afternoon when it began to blow rather violently, we headed for the ship. We were rowing for dear life when the ship moved so that we were in her lee, and then she floated a buoy downwind on a long warp. We grabbed the warp and pulled ourselves up to the ship. The boat we left half full of water, and were ourselves as wet as drowned rats. Still we did rejoice at having escaped that great peril. And all that night it blew a most violent gale of wind, with snow and hail.

About noon the next day, the 3rd, the wind moderated so we stood farther into the bay, anchoring in four and a half fathoms. We used our second anchor, because so many of the men were sick, and the rest so weakened that we could hardly raise our sheet-anchor. Presently I went ashore to see what comfort I could find. That was the first time that I put foot on that island, the island where we were destined to spend the winter. I noticed deer tracks and some fowl: but what excited me most was a break in the coastline that looked like the mouth of a river. We hurried over with great hopes but found the entrance to be solidly blocked by a sand-bar that was covered at high tide by only two feet of water. Yet inside the bar was a most excellent harbour with four fathom of water.[31] In the evening, when I returned aboard, I had nothing but hopes with which to comfort our sick men.

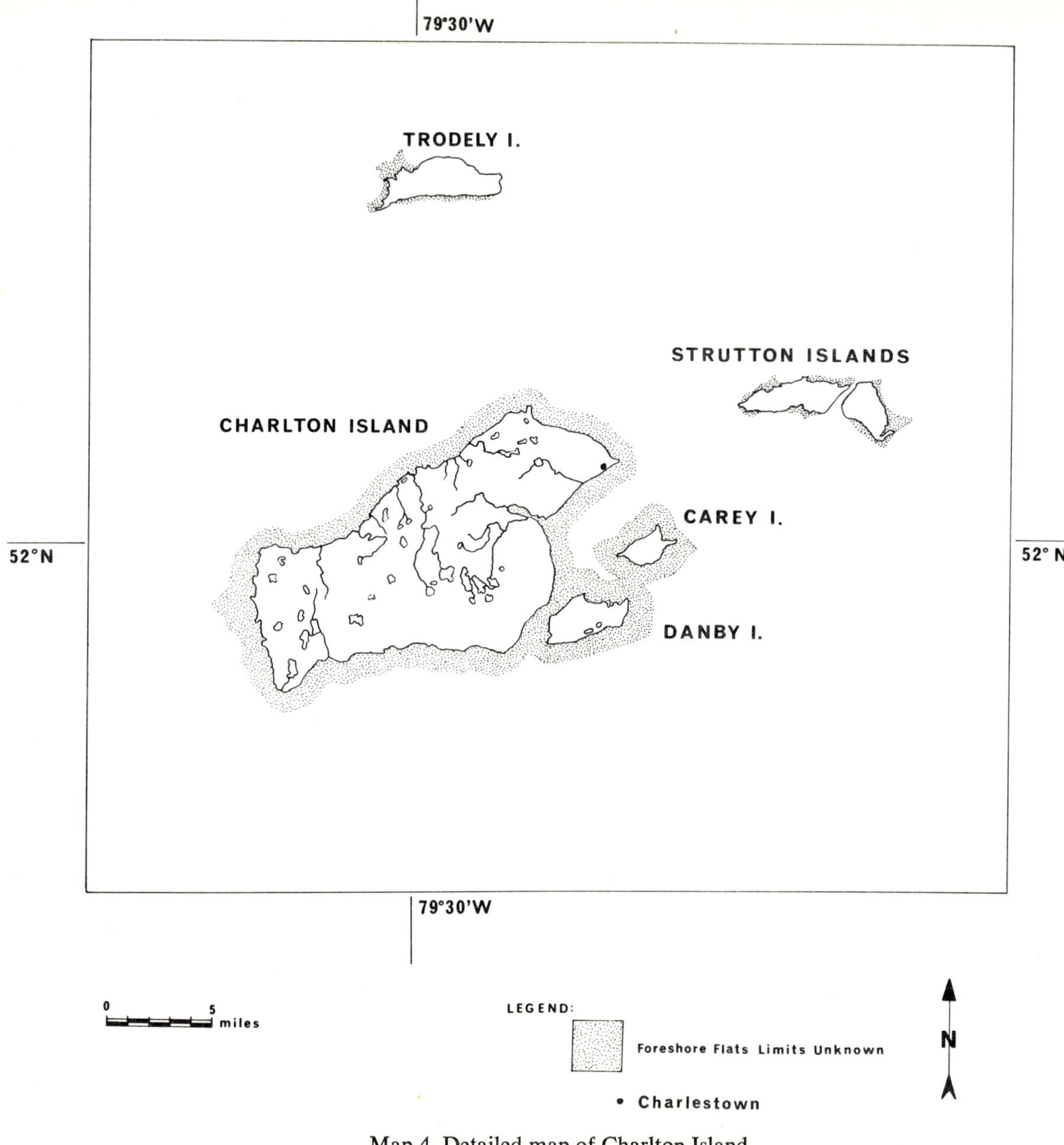


Map 4  Detailed map of Charlton Island

In spite of a heavy wind and a driving snow-storm on the 4th, I had
the men put me ashore, then go to take soundings at a place that
looked like a river-mouth. Meanwhile, with four of the men, I went
inland some four or five miles searching for anything that might help
the men in their illness, but could find only a few berries. After we
had exhausted ourselves in those troublesome woods, we returned
to the place where we were to meet the boat. I found that the men
had not gone exploring in my absence because it was impossible to
row against the fierce gale of wind that was blowing. Thus we returned, dejected, to our ship. The foul weather continued, with
snow, hail and very low temperatures till October 6th. Then, with
a favouring wind, we stood in closer to the shore and moored the
ship.

On the 7th, it snowed so heavily all day that we had to shovel it off
the decks while the storm roared about us. It continued snowing,
and it was so cold that the entire bow of the vessel, together with
the beak-head, was encased in ice that was half a foot thick, so
that we had to hew it off with axes. The anchor-cable, also, was so
heavily encased in ice that it was as thick as a man's waist. Although
the sun was shining brightly all day, it lacked the power to thaw
our sails. Finally we were forced to tear out each of the frozen top-
sails in a solid lump.

When everything was in order aboard the ship, we headed for shore.
We steered for the place where we had landed previously but could
not get near it because the snow and ice had formed such a thick
slush in the shallow water. This made it so difficult to row that
we could make no headway, even with four oars. Finally. however,
we got ashore a little farther to the westward. Because the weather
was becoming extremely cold and we had very little fuel aboard, I
had the men fill the boat with driftwood and take it to the ship. I
then sent the carpenter with some men to cut some fire-wood,
appointed others to carry it to the shore and had the boat bring it to
the vessel. For I suspected that the accumulating slush would soon
make it impossible for us to get ashore.

Already it was cold and miserable on the ship, with everything freezing in the hold, and even beside the fire itself. Seeing, therefore, that we could no longer make use of our sails—which are the very wings of a ship—it seemed almost certain that we would have to spend the winter locked in that frozen sea.

After we had brought aboard as much wood as we could conveniently stow (enough to last two or three months) the sick men asked me to build them a little house or hovel on the island, so that with better shelter they might regain their health. I took the carpenter, and some others whom I thought fit for such a task, and put them to work immediately. In the meantime I wandered up and down in the woods with some of the other men looking for signs of savages, so that I might better provide a defence against them. Fortunately we found no evidence that there were any savages at all on the island. By this time the snow was up to our knees, and stalking through it, we returned comfortless to our companions who had been working upon our house while we were away.

Meanwhile, the men on the ship had taken down the top-sails, built a hot fire on the hearth in the hatch-way and thawed them out. Then they folded them and put them below so that they would be ready for use if the weather improved. Thus we returned aboard in the evening. On the 12th, we took our main-sail from the yard—where it was frozen solid—thawed it out and carried it ashore to cover our house. By that night, they had covered it, and the six men who had built the house asked permission to spend the night there. I agreed to their proposal only after arming them with muskets and other furniture, and warning them to keep a sharp watch all night. In addition, they had with them the two greyhounds (a dog and a bitch) which I had brought from England to hunt deer, if we were lucky enough to find any.

By the following night, the 13th, our house was completed, and the men then asked me if they might go exploring. They left early the next morning with instructions to stay together and, above all else, to see if they could find some creek or cove where we could winter the ship. Meanwhile, the rest of us lowered our two top-masts with their rigging, after deciding that if we did find a place to winter the vessel, we could reach it with our fore-sail and mizzen. When the hunters returned on the 15th, they brought with them the carcass of a small, lean deer that they had killed. This cheered us up tremendously, as it raised the hope that we might get more fresh meat for our sick men. The hunters reported that they had wandered more than 20 miles from the house and that the deer had been shot about 12 miles away, at a spot where they had seen nine or ten more. Sleeping in the woods the night before had so chilled and weakened them that it took three or four days for them to recover. They saw no signs of savages or of any ravening wild beasts. Nor did they see any sign of a harbour where we might protect our ship.

Next my lieutenant and five of the men also wanted to explore the island to see what they could find. But they had even worse luck than the first party, for the snow had become very deep, making walking extremely difficult, and after spending a night in the bush they returned comfortless and miserably disabled from the cold. But what was more serious, they had lost one of the men, John Barton, the gunner's mate. Rather than go around a pond with the rest of the party, he had taken a short-cut across it—a distance of about a quarter of a mile. When he was in the middle of the pond, he went through the ice; the water closed over him and we never saw him again.[32] After this experience, I decided to fish no more with a golden hook,[33] for each hunting expedition weakened us so seriously that 20 such expensive deer would not restore us.

By this time, I felt certain that there were no savages upon our island or the neighbouring islands. Indeed, as they did not respond to the signal-fires that we made, it was very likely that there were none on the mainland either. Even if there were some savages about, the winter was so far advanced, and the weather so bad, that they couldn't reach us had they wanted to. So from then on, we comforted ourselves by sleeping more soundly. We changed the island garrison every week, and apart from that, expected no other diversion till spring.

From the 10th to the 29th, we had such frequent gales and blizzards that the boat seldom ventured away from the ship. When it did,

Plate 2  James' landing place on Charlton Island

Plate 3  Winter's Forest, where Charles Town was built

the men usually had to wade ashore through the heavy slush,
carrying one another. And each day we silently watched our condition grow more desperate. The blanket of snow on the island
became thicker and thicker, the temperature dropped steadily and
the slush along the shore became heavier and more impenetrable.
And only our most merciful God knew what would become of us.

On the 29th, I observed an eclipse of the moon. I exercised every
possible caution, both in regard to the precision of the instruments
and to the observation itself. The month of October ended with
heavy snow and bitterly cold weather.

**November, 1631**

With the steward, I took an inventory of our supplies on November
1st, for we had now been away from England for six months, or one
third of the proposed voyage. I found him to be an honest man. He
had given me an accounting each week of what supplies had been
used, and what remained in the hold under his care. And I made no
allowance for leakage or other waste unless he showed it to me at
the time. Every month I had had an inventory taken and now, after
six months, I put aside what remained of our allowance for that
period. This amounted to at least a month's supply of bread and a
two weeks' supply of peas and fish.

The boat tried to get ashore on the 3rd, but could not get through
the thick slush. On the 4th, they found a place where they could
get ashore, and between then and the 9th, they used it two or three
times to take beer to the men on shore. After one night in the house,
the beer would be frozen solid. When the frozen beer was thawed
in a kettle it was not good, so the men chopped holes through the
ice on the fresh-water ponds to get drinking-water. Because this
pond-water had a most vile smell, I thought it might be tainted, so
I had them dig a well near the house. There we got very good water
which tasted—or so we flattered ourselves—very much like milk.

On the 10th, having brought along a supply of planks for the purpose, I put the carpenter to work building a small boat. What I

wanted was a boat that we could carry over the ice and use in open
water should the occasion arise. At noon I measured the latitude
of the island with two quadrants and found that we were at 52° 00′
north. I urged the men to make fox traps, for we saw a number of
foxes every day. Some of them were dappled, black and white,
which led me to believe that there were some black foxes on the
island. I told the men that black fox-skins were extremely valuable
and that whoever caught one could keep the skin for his reward.
So the men made a variety of different traps which they could place
in the woods only by wading through very deep snow.

Our house caught fire on the 12th, but we soon put it out. We were
forced to keep a very big fire going day and night. But this accident
showed me that it was necessary to post a continual watch over the
fire, for if our house and clothing should be burnt we would be in
a most woeful condition. I stayed ashore till the 17th, while our
miserable circumstances grew steadily worse, with increasing snow
and ever lower temperatures. When we stood on the shore and
looked towards the ship, she looked like a piece of ice that had been
carved into the form of a ship. She was packed solidly in frozen
snow, while her bow and both sides were sheathed in ice. Our cables
froze in the hawse-holes and were strange indeed to behold. When I
returned aboard, I spent the long night being tormented by uncer-
tainty, and even in the light of day I could not see any way that I
could save the ship. Only one thing was certain: it was impossible to
endure such extremities much longer. Every day the men had to
beat the ice off the cables, and to dig the ice out of the hawse-holes
with the carpenter's long caulking-iron. While they were doing
this, the water would freeze on their clothes and hands, and would
make them so numb that they could hardly climb back aboard
without being heaved up on the end of a rope.

On the 19th, our gunner—who, as you may remember, had his leg
cut off—was dying. By now he had grown extremely weak and
asked that he might be permitted to drink as much sherry as he
wanted for the little time he had to live. I granted his wish and he
died on the morning of November 22nd. He was a brave and
honest man who had a tight little bunk in the gun-room, with all the

blankets he wanted (for there was no shortage), a pan of coals and a fire that burned continually. In spite of that, his bandage would freeze on his wound, and his bottle of sherry at his head. We committed his body to the sea at a good distance from the ship.

On the 23rd, there was much more ice on the bay; and when the snow fell on the water the individual flakes just floated there instead of melting. Much ice drifted past the ship all day, but it was soft, crumbly stuff—just frozen slush. But in the evening, after the watch was set, a large slab of ice came obliquely across our bow, quickly followed by four others. The smallest of them must have been a quarter of a mile wide, and we were astonished to see them float silently against us out of the darkness. We were certain they would carry us out of the harbour and into the rocks and shoals to the east. For these were no longer cakes of congealed slush, but large floes of newly formed, solid ice about two inches thick. Fortunately, they couldn't dislodge us. Rather, the floes broke against us and the pieces drifted away. But the anchor and cable had to endure incredible stresses, sometimes stopping the whole ice-floe. We fired three muskets as a signal to the men on shore that we were in distress. They answered our signal, but there was no way they could come to our assistance. And by ten o'clock the ice had disappeared and we were out of danger.

We still kept a very careful watch, however, and our labours were made more comfortable by weather that was the warmest we had experienced during the whole month of November. At dawn the next morning, I sent for the men who were in the house on shore. With great difficulty, they arrived about ten o'clock, after being forced to wade through the slush along the shore. That day, many floes of ice drifted past the ship. They were not nearly as large as the ones of the previous night, but they were much thicker. Once some pieces fouled the cable and made the ship drag her anchor.

As soon as we were clear of it, we manned the winch and raised the easternmost anchor, for I was now resolved to run the ship aground because neither cables nor anchors could hold her. But first, let me explain to you why I didn't run her aground earlier. First, the

whole area was very rocky, with many rocks sticking up three or
four feet out of the water. Second, the usual tide there was not
over two and a half feet, so that if she were to bed down deep in
the sand we would never be able to dig her out because she would
also be under four or five feet of water. Third, the whole coast was
loose sand which might be piled up around the ship so high that we
would not be able to move it in the spring. Fourth, we doubted
that the tides would run as high in the spring as they did in the fall.
Fifth, we had no way of protecting her from the tides which ran
fairly swiftly along the shore. Exposed to those tidal currents, she
might be buried under the ice or torn apart so that her planks and
iron-works would be carried away. And if our ship did not survive,
we needed those parts to build a pinnace. Sixth, if we had a storm
out of the northwest, we would have a tide of at least 10 feet. This
high tide, with a northwest or offshore wind, would clear away all
the ice and raise a violent surf over the shoal water around the
point to the east of us. This turbulence would make the vessel
pound violently, and if she were beached by that surf, or any heavy
sea, it was very doubtful that we would ever get her off again.

It was for these various reasons that we had endured so many
extremities, while we hoped for some good and fortunate accident.
But by now we saw that our hopes were simply foolish, and that
a great deal of our miserable labour had been totally in vain. So
with the flood we weighed our westernmost anchor, noting God's
manifest assistance therein, because it happened to be fine, warm
weather, without which we would not have been able to work.
The wind was now from the south, an onshore wind, and the one
that raised the lowest tides. We brought the ship into 12 feet of
water, and laid out two anchors, one in the offing and one towards
the land, so we could draw her ashore at a moment's notice. We
hoped, also, that some stones to the westward would fend off some
of the ice. We were then about a mile from the shore. About ten
o'clock, in pitch blackness, the ice came driving down upon us and
tore out our anchors. The ship drifted some two cable-lengths[34]
before the brisk south wind, and by two o'clock was firmly aground.
Although some ice piled up against us, she lay quietly all night,
and we took some rest.

On the 25th, the wind shifted to the east and piled great heaps of
ice against us. At high tide, we manned the capstan, drawing home
our anchors by main force while we tried to encourage one another.
We were trying to drag the ship through great pieces of ice and
onto the shore. But to our great distress, when the tide was about
half way in (or about two hours before high tide) the ship was
driven into the ice to the eastward, and it looked as though she was
about to be driven onto the rocks in spite of all our efforts. As I
mentioned earlier, the last couple of days had been very warm,
with some rain (only the second rain we had had since arriving at
the island), and without such fine weather we could have done
nothing. In addition, the wind suddenly shifted again to the south
and at the very same instant blew a hard puff which lasted half an
hour. I brought the two top-sails from between the decks where
they were stored, and quickly hoisted them up with ropes. Thus we
drove the vessel ashore when she was only half a cable-length from
the rocks.

In the evening we broke a path through the ice and put an anchor
out towards the shore in five feet of water. This was to keep the ship
from being swept out to sea if at all possible. There, Sir Hugh Willoughby[35] came to mind, for without doubt he was driven out of his
harbour in a similar situation and starved to death at sea. But God
was more merciful to us. About nine o'clock that night, the wind
shifted to the northwest and blew up a storm. Being off the shore,
this wind blew all the ice out to sea long before we were afloat.
Then there came a great rolling sea around the point, which raised
a heavy surf along the shore. And we were aground and at the
mercy of that sea. By ten o'clock she began to roll at her moorings,
and shortly after began to pound against the bottom.

I put as many men at the capstan as there was room for, and put
other men at the pumps, for we thought that every fifth or sixth
blow would have stove her in. At the capstan, we heaved with all our
strength to keep her as solidly grounded as possible. There being
a very high tide because of the wind, we drew the ship up so high
that it was doubtful if we would ever get her off again. Still she
continued pounding till two o'clock the next morning, when she

Plate 4  Reef off the northeast point of Charlton Island

finally settled. At this point we fell into an exhausted sleep for we
expected to be tormented again with the next tide.

At high tide the next morning, the 26th, our ship remained firmly
grounded so we had some peace. After prayers, I called a con-
ference of the master, my lieutenant, the mates, the carpenter
and the boatswain. I pointed out that our situation was desperate,
and I wanted them to tell me what they though of my proposal. I
suggested that we carry all our provisions ashore and then, when
the wind shifted to the north, winch the ship out into deeper water
and sink her. After much discussion, they agreed to my proposal.
I then informed the men of our decision, and they too agreed with it.

And so we set to work. That day we took ashore two dryfats[36] of
bread and a hogshead of beef, having much trouble pushing the
boat through the slush. And in the evening, the wind, coming out
of the northeast and east, choked the bay with ice. On the 27th,
the bay continued to be full of ice, which made it impossible for us
to land anything, and I hoped that the ice would remain there and
freeze solid so that we would not be forced to sink our ship. At
dawn the next day, three of the men went ashore over the ice without my knowledge. Then a west wind drove most of the ice from
between the ship and the shore, as well as other parts of the bay.
But it was still not sufficiently cleared that we could send a boat
ashore.

I saw now that we would have to sink the vessel with the first north
or northwest wind, so I had the carpenter get everything ready. On
the starboard side, towards the stern, I had him cut a four- or five-
inch square through the interior planking some four feet above
the keel. With the exterior planking thus exposed, it could be bored
through in an instant. Then we moved the bread from the bread-
room to the main cabin where we also put our gun-powder. Much
of our light dry materials were taken out of the hold, and placed
between decks.

On the 29th, at five o'clock in the morning, it began to blow very
hard from the west northwest. Ordinarily, such a wind would shift

clockwise through the north, so I prepared for our sinking. I sent
the cooper down into the hold with orders to drive in the bungs of
the full casks and to bring the empty ones on deck, or, if that was
not possible, to stave them in. I had all our cables coiled upon our
lower tire,[37] and then piled on all of our spare anchors and other
heavy objects to keep it from floating. By seven o'clock, it was
blowing a gale from the northwest, a bitterly adverse wind. The ship
was already bedded some two feet into the sand, and so long as the
gale continued from the same quarter, she would pound on the
bottom. In my previous considerations, I had thought she was
driven so hard aground that we might never get her off. Yet we had
been so ferreted by her last beating that I resolved to sink her right
there rather than expose her to the hazard of another beating.

By nine o'clock, she began to roll because of an extraordinary
great sea that was running. And then was the fatal hour that drove
us to the end of our wits. So I went down into the hold with the
carpenter, took his auger and bored a hole in the ship to let in the
water. Then, with all speed, we began to bore holes in other places,
but every other place was full of nails. By ten o'clock, however,
the lower tire was covered with water. In spite of that, the ship
began to pound so heavily that we could neither work nor stand
in her. Nor would she sink as quickly as we would have liked.
With each wave, she would pound first her stern then her bows with
such violence that it was wonderful how she endured even a quarter
of an hour of such punishment. By twelve o'clock her lower tire
was afloat, and pounding her from the inside with such violence
that it stove in the bulk-heads of the bread-room and the powder-
room as well as the fore-piece. And when the water rose between
the decks, the chests stored there were dashed wildly about, and the
water itself surged back and forth till we expected it to split the
vessel wide open. At one o'clock the constant pounding broke off
her rudder, which disappeared in the surf.

Thus she continued pounding till three o'clock: then the sea rose
above her upper deck, and shortly after she began to settle. With
the ship, we were forced to sink the greater part of our bedding and
clothes, as well as the surgeon's chest. Meanwhile, the men on

shore stood watching us, almost dead from the cold and the misery
which we shared. We looked at each other with woeful hearts. As
the dark of night drew on, I had the boat made ready, and ordered
my loving companions to leave the sunken vessel. The men, express-
ing their faithful affection for me, seemed reluctant to leave until I
told them that I intended to go ashore with them. And thus, at last,
I abandoned my ship.

We were 17 poor souls now in the boat, and we suspected that we
had leapt out of the frying-pan into the fire. For the tide was
ebbing and the slush was so thick that we thought we would be
swept out to sea. We therefore double-manned four oars, had four
others standing by and with the help of God got ashore and pulled
the boat up on the beach. One thing was most strange to see in
that thick, slushy water—there was a great, swelling sea! On landing
we greeted our companions as best we could but we could not
recognize them, nor they us, because our faces, hair and clothing
were all coated with ice.

And now I would like to pause in this long and unpleasant story
to make a few general observations. Since our arrival at the bottom
of the bay, the winds have been very unsteady and variable; and
except for the past fortnight, the coldest winds have been from the
south. I think that this is because the south wind blew from the
mainland which was covered with snow, while the north wind came
from the bay which was still open water. Being under a south bank
also gave us greater protection from the north wind, so that we
may not have noticed it so much. If a gale was blowing from the
northwest, northwest by north or north northwest, it would raise
an unusually high tide. With the wind in the opposite direction,
there would be little tidal movement, and the harder it blew the less
tide there would be. With little wind or a dead calm, there was a
tide of some three feet. But with the northwest winds mentioned
above, the tide could rise to 10 feet. I could see no difference
between neap and spring tides.

# Our Wintering on Charlton Island

After beaching the boat, we followed the shore in the dark to our house, where we built a great fire to thaw ourselves out and comforted ourselves with bread and water. Then, after I had told the men that each one should speak his mind freely, we began to discuss the fate of our ship. The carpenter, particularly, was of the opinion that she would never sail again. He said that she had been pounded so unmercifully that all her fastenings would be loose and her seams opened. There was not enough tide to careen the ship, nor was there any cove or creek in the area where she might be grounded for repairs. Moreover, he pointed out that she had lost her rudder and he had no iron-work to build another. Some of the men thought that we had grounded her so solidly that we would never get her afloat again; others thought that because she was exposed to the tidal currents, the ice would probably tear her to pieces. And in addition, our two remaining anchors were buried under the ice and we had no way of retrieving them. Thus, we would have no anchors to get us safely home even if we got the ship afloat and she proved seaworthy.

I comforted the men as best I could with a statement such as this:

My master and faithful companions, be not dismayed about any of these possible disasters, but let us put our entire trust in God. It is He that giveth and He that taketh away. He casts down with one hand and raiseth up with another. His will be done. If it be our fate to end our days here, we are as close to heaven as we would be in England.[38] And we are fortunate that God Almighty has given us so great a time for repentance, for he calls upon us daily to prepare ourselves for a better life in Heaven. I have no doubt that He will be merciful to us both here on earth and in His blessed kingdom.

Meanwhile, we may use every honest means to save and prolong our natural lives. In my judgement, we are not yet beyond all hope of returning to our native land. And I see a way in which we might just do it. Let us admit that the ship might be lost, which God forbid; yet some of our own country-men —as well as others—have survived similar extremities. They have built a pinnace out of the wreckage of their own vessel and so returned to their friends. It might be objected that these things happened in warmer climates and more open seas, and to crews that had an abundance of fresh food. And this is so. Yet there is nothing too difficult for courageous men, as you have already shown, and beyond doubt will continue to show.

The men all offered to work to the limits of their strength and to carry out any order that I might give them, no matter how hazardous. I thanked them all. For his cheerful offer to build a pinnace, I promised to give the carpenter as much plate, presently, as would be worth 10 pounds sterling. And if it should be that I sailed to England in the pinnace, he could have her when we got there, and would also be given 50 pounds in money. I also promised that all men who were careful and industrious would also be rewarded. Thus we resolved to build a new pinnace with the timber we should get upon the island; in the spring, if we found that the ship was not serviceable, we would break her up and use her planks to sheathe our new vessel. And so we settled ourselves close about the fire and took some rest till daylight.

On November 30th, early in the morning, I had the surgeon give me a shave and a haircut because I was collecting so many icicles that it was intolerable. The rest of the men followed my example. I then divided the men into three groups and arranged to bring our clothes and provisions ashore. The master with one gang of men, was to go aboard the vessel to get things out of the hold. The coxswain, with another gang, was to ferry the gear ashore in the boat. With the rest of the men, I would carry it half a mile through the snow to the place where we intended to build a store-house. The heavier things we simply left on the beach. By the afternoon, the wind had veered to the south southwest, and the water ebbed so low that we thought we might get something out of our hold. We therefore launched the boat and I sent it out to the ship through the thick, congealed slush. It was extremely cold as I stood on the shore convinced that, with the tide, the boat would be carried out to sea and then we would all be lost. But by God's assistance, they got safely to the ship, and built a fire there to signal their arrival aboard. They fell presently to work and carried some supplies out of the hold and up to the decks. Then, as night was fast approaching, they did not dare to come ashore, but lay on the bed in the main cabin almost frozen.

## December, 1631

December 1st was so cold that I walked to the ship over the ice, following the same path that the boat had taken the day before. We carried ashore bundles containing 500 of our fish, and much of our bedding and clothes, which we were forced to dig out of the ice in the ship. The weather was so mild on the 2nd, however, that some of the men who were going over the ice fell in and barely recovered: so, as we could land nothing either by boat or on our backs, I put the men to building a store-house ashore. In the evening, a west wind broke up the ice and drove it out of the bay. This was thick ice in large slabs, and could very easily have wrecked the ship.

On the 3rd, several great slabs of ice came to rest against the side of the ship, but we were unable to reach the ship by climbing over them. We found a way for the boat to reach her, but when loaded she drew four feet of water and could not get within a bow-shot of the shore. The men, therefore, had to wade through the thick, heavy slush, carrying everything from the boat to the shore on their backs. Every time they waded in the water, it froze about them so that they looked like walking pieces of ice and were most lamentable to behold. That evening they attempted to hoist the boat aboard the ship, because the extreme cold made it unlikely that they could use it any longer to ferry supplies ashore. So they cut away as much ice from the boat as they could and with hand-spikes picked it out of the bilges. But, in spite of all they could do, the boat was still too heavy to be hoisted aboard, and they were forced to leave her in the tackles by the ship's side.

The 4th being Sunday, we rested and performed the Sabbath duties of Christians.

The 5th and 6th were extremely cold, but we made bags out of our stock of spare shirts and used them to carry our loose bread ashore. We also dug new sails and clothes out of the ice with iron hand-spikes and carried them ashore, where we dried them out by a big fire. The next day was so bitterly cold that our noses, cheeks and hands were frozen as white as paper. Both the 8th and 9th were still cold, and with much snow, yet we continued our labour of carrying and ferrying our gear ashore. In the evening, on a very high tide, the ice smashed two of the thwarts in the boat and stove in her side. At the time there was nothing we could do about it.

On the 10th the carpenter found suitable timber to make a keel and stern-post for our pinnace. The rest of us worked at getting more provisions ashore until the 13th, which we spent digging the boat out of the ice. In doing so we were forced to dig right down to her keel, as well as chip the ice out of her bilges; and when we got her up on the ice, many of our men had their noses, cheeks and fingers frozen. And still it grew colder. By the 19th, we could get nothing more out of the hold, being forced to leave behind five barrels of beef and pork, all of our beer and sundry other things that were frozen solidly into the ship. And the 21st was so cold that we could not even go out of the house. On the 23rd, we went to bring our boat ashore, running her over the oars which we used as skids, but by ten o'clock there was such a thick fog that it was as dark as night. I made the men abandon the boat and head for shore, which was difficult to do because the men kept getting separated and lost in the dark. At last we all met at the house inconceivably frozen and miserable. Upon many of the men, the cold raised blisters as big as walnuts, probably because they went too hastily to the fire.

Our well was now so frozen that though we dug as deep as we could, we could find no water and were forced to use melted snow. Now melted snow is very unwholesome, either to drink or to use in preparing food, and it also made us so short of breath that we were scarcely able to talk. All of our sack, vinegar, oil and other liquids were frozen as solid as blocks of wood, and indeed we had to cut them with a hatchet. Our house was all covered with frost and ice on the inside, and anything that was three feet or more from the fire

was frozen solid. When I first landed upon that island, I had found
a spring at the foot of a hill about three-quarters of a mile from
our house. At the time, I had the men cut down some trees to mark
the spot so that we could find it again. Now, on the 24th, I sent
three of the men who had been with me at the time to see if it was
still flowing. Wading through the snow, the men finally located a
small trickle of water, and shovelling away the snow, made their
way to its source. They found the spring to be bubbling strongly
from the earth, and brought me a can of it for which I was very
thankful. All through the winter, the spring continued to flow, and
though it froze slightly at the surface, we could always break
through this film of ice and come to fresh, clear water.

For the past three or four days, we had worked very hard to get
fire-wood to the house, which was a very troublesome task because
of the deep snow. We then arranged our bedding and provisions so
we could keep Christmas day holy and solemnized in the most
joyful manner possible. We celebrated St. John's Day in a similar
fashion, and also by naming the woods where we had built our little
settlement, "Winter's Forest," in memory of that honourable knight,
Sir John Winter.[39] And now instead of a Christmas tale, I will
describe the house we were living in, as well as the adjoining
structure.

When I first resolved to build a house, I chose the warmest and best
place that was close to the ship. It was in a stand of big trees,
under a south bank, about a bow-shot from the shore. First, we
tried to dig a hole or cave in the earth—which would have been
the best protection—but that project failed when we struck water
within two feet of the surface. As the soil there was a white,
light sand, we had no way of building a mud wall: nor could we use
stones, as there were none in the area, and those that might have
been available from farther away were already covered with snow.
And as we had no planks, we were forced, therefore, to do the
best we could with such materials as we had around us.

The house we built was about 20 feet square, or as large, roughly,
as would be covered by the main-sail of our ship. First we drove

strong stakes into the earth, and wattled them as thickly as possible
with boughs which we beat down very tightly. This, the first house
we put up, was six feet high on both sides; but at the ends, the stakes
rose almost up to the ridge-pole where we left two holes for the
light to come in and the smoke to go out.[40] Next we fastened a
rough tree aloft for the ridge-pole on which we laid our rafters.
Over that, we stretched our main course which, lying athwart,
reached down to the ground on both sides. And thus was it built.

On the inside we fastened our bonnets[41] all the way around. Then
we drove in stakes to make bunk frames around three sides of the
house. The bunks were double, one above the other, with the lower
one being a foot from the ground. We filled them with boughs
which we covered with spare sails, and then spread our bedding.
In the middle of the house was the hearth and on it we built our
fire. Some boards were laid around the hearth to stand on, to protect our feet from the cold and dampness. From our waist cloths[42]
and small sails we fashioned canopies and curtains.

Our second house was not more than 20 feet away from the first
and was wattled in a similar manner, but it was smaller because it
was covered by our fore-course. It had no piles of wood on the
south side, but in lieu of that we stacked up all our chests along
the inside of the wall. And, indeed, the heat of the fire was reflected
back by the chests, making this house warmer than our dwelling. We
used this house to prepare our food in, and for the men to lounge
around in during the day if they had nothing else to do.

A third house was located some 20 paces from the second, for fear
of fire. This—a storehouse—was nothing but a ridge-pole, with
rafters laid from it to the ground, and covered with a new set of
sails. The floor was partially covered with poles on which we placed
a two-foot layer of boughs; on this we stored our fish and bread, so
as to preserve them better. Other things were just piled in anywhere.

Long before Christmas our bunk-house was covered almost to
the roof with snow, as was our cook-house. But our store-house was
completely covered because it was unheated. Thus we lived in a
heap and wilderness of snow. We could not go outside, unless we

followed the short paths which we kept cleared. In one place we
had a special path about ten steps long, which we used for exercis-
ing the men, and where I took my own exercise. To make this, we
first shovelled away the snow, then packed it down with our feet till
it was fairly hard. And when we had finished we still had three feet
of snow under us. Each day we worked on both houses and walks,
to make them more comfortable and more suitable to our purposes.

On the 27th, we got our boat ashore, and carried some of our
provisions from the beach to the store-house. And so, by degrees,
we carried all of our provisions to the store-house, keeping the
path open by shovelling out the snow, and performing this labour
while we suffered painfully from the cold. And thus we concluded
the old year—1631.

**January, 1632**

The 1st of January, and indeed most of the month, was extremely
cold. On the 6th I checked our latitude as precisely as I could—it
was a clear, sunny day—and found it to be 51° 52′ north. The
difference between this and our previous calculations is caused by
refraction. On the 21st I saw the sun rising like an oval along the
horizon and called three or four of the men to see it, so as to confirm
my judgement. We agreed that it was twice as long as it was broad.
We plainly saw that as it rose up higher above the horizon it
gradually recovered its roundness. I noted, too, that when the
eastern edge of the moon touched the planet Mars, on the 26th, the
Lion's Heart was then in the east quarter 21° 45′ above the horizon.
This however, was not done with the precision of my other observations.

Late in the evening of both the 30th and 31st, there were almost
twice as many stars in the sky as I had ever seen before. I could see
that the Cloud in Cancer was full of small stars, as were the
Pleiades, while the whole Milky Way was nothing but a streak of
tiny stars. When the moon came up about ten o'clock, a quarter of
the stars disappeared. The wind was northerly throughout most of
the month, and very cold. Whenever it was warm enough, we kept

Plate 5  Wind-packed and sculptured snow

busy by fetching wood, working on the pinnace, and other things that needed to be done. Early in the month the sea became solidly frozen, so that no open water was visible in any direction. I hope it will not seem tedious to the reader if I now give my own opinion as to how this abundance of ice is formed.

The land that encircles this great bay is for the most part low and flat and is edged with half a mile to a mile of shoals that are dry at low tide. The bay itself is a shattered, irregular thing with many shoal bays and guts, and is sprinkled with islands and sand-banks. About the middle of September, the rains of summer are suddenly replaced by snow which no longer melts but simply collects on the land. When it snows at low water, as it does very often, it covers the shore. Then, twice every 24 hours, the tide officiously carries this snow out into the great bay where it collects. Every low water, the sands are left clean to gather more snow to add to the collection that is floating in the bay. Thus more and more snow is collected.

About the end of October, this collection of floating snow has chilled the water of the bay to the point where falling snow doesn't melt in the water, but floats on the surface without even changing colour. The wind gathers this floating snow together, and as the winter advances it begins to freeze, as much as two or three inches thick in one night. As it is carried around with the tide, it will sooner or later run against some obstacle which crumples it and piles it upon itself so that in a few hours it will be five or six feet thick. The tide, still flowing, carries it away so fast that by December it has grown to an infinite multiplication of ice. And thus, through the collecting and storing of this ice, the cold becomes predominant in the sea. And because the sea furnishes those low lands with springs and waters, it slowly cools the land also. That is what we have learned through our experience, though in all of this I freely submit myself to those who are better educated.

My men were more mortified by the cold when wading through the water in early June, when the sea was full of ice, than they were in December when the ice was just forming. And our well which was flowing freely in December was bone-dry in July. Now, in January,

the ground was frozen to a depth of 10 feet. Now the vast quantity
of ice may be calculated very easily by mathematical demonstration,
yet it is my opinion that the bay does not freeze over completely:
for on the 21st, with a gale blowing from the north, we could see
the ice rising and falling in the bay.

## February, 1632

This month, the cold was as severe as anything we had felt. And by
now many of the men were complaining of infirmities. Some had
sore mouths and loose teeth, and gums so swollen with rotten flesh
that the surgeon had to cut it away daily. The pain was so severe
that they could not eat their regular food. Some complained of pains
in their heads and chests, some of a weakness in their backs and
others of aches in their thighs and knees, while still others had
swellings in their legs. Although two-thirds of the men were under
the surgeon's care, they still had to go outside every day to fetch
wood and timber. As it was, most of them had no shoes to wear, for
when they came in out of the cold, they would crowd so closely
around the fire, that their shoes burned and scorched on their feet;
and our spare shoes were all sunk with the ship. In this extremity,
the men bound their feet with scraps of cloth or leather and then
performed their duties as best they could. The carpenter, too, had
fallen sick by this time, to our great dismay.

I made some observations on the rising and setting of the sun,
calculating the time of these events by some very accurate glasses.
Although we kept our clock and watch wrapped up in cloth in a
chest by the fire, they were so frozen that they stopped. My observations by these glasses I compared with the meridian transits of some
stars. By this means I found that the sun rose 20 minutes early and
set some 20 minutes late because of refraction.

Since I have spoken so much of the cold, I hope that the reader
will not take it too coldly if I try to describe it briefly. We recog-
nized three different kinds of cold, which we experience in three
different places—in the house, in the woods and on the ice when
we were going to the ship. The last was certainly the worst. On the

ice the cold would sometimes be so extreme as to be almost unendurable. No clothes were proof against it, and no motion could resist it. Moreover, it would freeze together the hair on our eyelids till we could not see. And I truly believe that it would have stifled a man in a very few hours.

Experience taught us—and reminded us each day—that the cold in the woods would freeze our faces or any patch of exposed skin. Yet it was not so mortifying as the cold on the ice. Our house was two-thirds covered with snow on the outside, and on the inside was frozen and festooned with icicles. In the morning, the clothes on our beds would be covered with hoar-frost, although the beds in that little dwelling were not far from the fire. But let us move even closer. The tubs that the cook used for thawing out the meat stood about a yard from the fire, and all day he would ply it with melted snow. Yet during the night, while the cook slept a single watch, the tubs would freeze solid. He was forced, then, to thaw his meat in a brass kettle very close to the fire. And many times I have seen—and felt by sticking my hand into it—that the side nearest the fire was very warm, while the other side was covered by an inch of ice. I leave further description to the cook who has an almost miraculous view of that cold.

The surgeon, who had hung his bottles of syrups and other liquids as close to the fire as possible so as to preserve them, had them all frozen. And our vinegar, oil and sack, which we kept in small casks in the house, were frozen solid. More broadly, we may note that the sea-ice was not yet broken up in early June. Moreover, when we tried to bury our dead and erect the King's standard towards the end of June, we found that the ground was still frozen. And when we left the island in early July, our well was still frozen, although the weather was very hot.

**March, 1632**

As the 1st of March was St. David's Day, we kept holiday and solemnized it in the manner of the ancient Britons, praying for the happiness of His Highness, Charles, Prince of Wales. On the 15th

one of the men thought that he saw a deer. With my permission, he
set out with two or three companions to see if he could shoot it.
They returned that evening so disabled with cold that they had
blisters the size of walnuts on the soles of their feet and on their
legs. In a fortnight, they had still not recovered to their former state
of health, which, incidentally, was not very good. On the 26th
three other men went hunting and returned even more seriously
disabled than the first group, and almost stifled with the cold. That
evening, the moon rose in a very flat oval along the horizon.

By the end of the month, the carpenter had set up 17 ground timbers and 34 staddles,[43] and was doing the best he could—poor
man—although he had to be led to his work. Briefly, then, the
entire month was very cold, with the wind usually from the northwest and the snow as deep as it had been all winter. Many people
would think that if we were living in a forest, we should have no
trouble keeping warm. It is true that we lived in a forest, and under
a south bank, too, or else we would surely have frozen to death.
For I can tell you how difficult it was to collect fire-wood in that
forest. But first, let me tell you about the tools we had. The carpenter did indeed have two axes in his tool-chest, but one of these
had been broken when we were cutting wood to pile about our
house before Christmas. When we first came ashore, we had but
two complete hatchets, and in a few days both of them had been
broken off two inches below their sockets. At that point, I called for
three of the cooper's hatchets and locked up the best one together
with the carpenter's axe. I had new handles put in the other two
hatchets, and set the two broken blades into cleft pieces of wood
that were bound as tightly as possible with strands of rope which
had to be renewed daily. And those were the only cutting tools we
had.

Moreover, as early as February 6th, the carpenter's best axe was
broken two inches below the socket when one of the men handled it
indiscreetly. After that we had to make use of those broken tools
as best we could. I therefore ordered that the carpenter should have
one of the cooper's hatchets; the men who were searching for ship's
timbers in the forest should have the other; and the men who cut

Plate 6  Charlton Sound in February

fire-wood were to have the two pieces that were bound in cleft sticks. And all this had happened before Christmas!

The three men who were appointed to look for naturally curved ship's timber in the forest had to stalk and wade through the snow —sometimes on all fours. And when they found a tree that seemed likely to fit the pattern, they first had to heave away the snow to see if it would in fact be suitable. If not, they must seek further. If it did fit the pattern they had to build a fire to thaw it out, otherwise it could not be cut. Then they had to cut it down, cut it off the length of the pattern, and with the help of some additional men, carry it home through a mile of snow.

We could not burn green wood in the fire because of the smoke which was so bad that the men would rather freeze outside than endure it. Even the dry wood was bad enough, for it was full of turpentine and sent forth such a thick smoke that it deposited an abundance of soot on everything in the house. This made us all look as if we were members of the Company of Chimney-Sweeps. Our clothes were burned full of holes, and most of us were without shoes. But let us get back to our wood-cutters again. They had to wander around in the snow till they saw a dead tree that was stand-ing, for the fallen ones were buried in the snow. Then they had to hack it down with their broken hatchets so that others could carry it home through the snow.

With their cutlasses, the boys had to cut up brush for the carpenter because every piece of timber that he shaped had to be thawed out first in the fire: the carpenter himself had to have a fire beside him continually or he could not work. And that was our constant labour throughout that terrible cold, besides tending the sick, and other chores.


**April, 1632**

April 1st was Easter, which we celebrated as religiously as God did give us grace. Easter, as well as the two following holy days, was

extremely cold, so we sat around the fire and discussed our situation.
We had five men, including the carpenter, who were not able to
do anything. The boatswain and several others were very infirm,
and of the remainder there were only five men who could eat their
ordinary rations. While the time of year moved swiftly forward, the
weather improved hardly at all. Our pinnace was making only
indifferent progress, while the carpenter grew worse and worse. And
our ship (as we then thought) was filled with solid ice that was
heavy enough to open the seams of even a new and sturdy vessel.
In brief, after many arguments and a frank discussion of our miserable condition, I resolved upon this course: I decided that with the
first warm weather we would clear the ship of ice, and we would
do this in spite of the additional labour and the fact that we were
growing steadily weaker.

Following that decision, we examined the tools that were available
for digging the ice out of the ship. Ashore we had but two iron bars,
one of which was broken, while the rest were sunk in the ship. So
we set to work repairing the iron bars, as well as the four broken
shovels that we had. With these meagre tools we intended (as later
we did) to dig the ice out of our ship and to pile it upon our port
bow. The weight of this pile would sink the ice to the bottom where
it would act as a barricade during the break-up which we were
afraid might smash our ship.

On the 6th we had the heaviest snow-fall of the year, one that filled
all of the paths that led into the forest. This snow was moister and
coarser than any we had had that winter: formerly it had been dry
and as fine as sand, and would float like dust before the wind. This
severe weather continued until the 15th, at which time our spring
was frozen more solidly than it had been all winter. I had often
observed that misty weather caused a greater refraction than did
clear weather. For example, from a low hill near our house we
could never see a small island situated about four leagues off to the
south southeast, if the weather was clear and sunny. But if the
weather was misty, we could often see it, even from sea-level. I had
seen the little island the previous year when I was on Danby Island.

With my instrument I measured the height of that little island on
the 13th, while I was standing near the shore, and found it to be
34′ minutes when the sun was 28° high. This shows how great the
refraction is in that area. Incidentally, I have seen the land elevated
because of refraction, and at the same time have seen the sun rise
perfectly round.

The 16th was the most comfortable and sunny day we had seen, so
I put some of the men to work clearing the snow from the upper
decks of the ship. Then I had them clear out the main cabin, and
start a fire to dry it out. Meanwhile, I had other men dig down
through the ice to see if they could find our anchor which was in
shoal water, and by the afternoon of the 17th, it had been located
and carried aboard. On the 18th, I had the men dig through the ice
at the spot where we thought the rudder might be. They dug
through to water, but could not find the rudder. We were afraid
that it might already have been buried in the sand, or even that it
might already have been carried away by the ice. But if it was still
there, we had to find it by digging through the ice, for it would
surely be carried away at break-up.

On the 19th we continued mining the ice in our ship but returned
in the evening to have supper ashore. The master and two of the
men, however, requested permission to spend the night aboard, and
I granted their request because they had spent a very uncomfortable winter through sharing their beds with the sick, as I myself
had done. By spending the night on the ship, they avoided the
necessity of listening to the pitiful groans and lamentations of the
sick men who were enduring intolerable torments, poor souls.

By the 21st our labours were so successful that we had located a
cask in the hold, and had also determined that there was water in
the hold beneath the ice. We knew that the water could not have
come from melted ice in the ship, because everything was still
frozen solid, both day and night, aboard ship as well as on land.
On the evening of the 23rd, we tapped the cask we had located and
found that it was full of very good beer. We were all extremely
pleased with our luck, especially the men who were sick, and this

in spite of the fact that the beer tasted slightly of bilge-water. It was
the taste of the beer that led us to believe that the holes we had cut
to sink the ship were frozen shut, and that the bilge-water in the
hold had been there all winter. But when we went to work on the
morning of the 24th, we found that the water had risen two feet
above the level of the ice where we had stopped work earlier. This
high water was caused by a north wind which had blown all night
and raised a higher tide than usual.

When the wind shifted to the south the next morning, we expected,
with very little reason, that the tide might drop very low. I therefore put the men to digging through the ice on the outside of the
ship to see if we could uncover the lower hole that we had cut
through the hull towards the stern. By working well into the night,
we dug down through the ice and found that it was unfrozen, as it
had been all winter. And to our great comfort, we found that inside
the ship, the water had dropped to the level of the hole, and on the
outside, it was a foot lower. To see if water entered the ship by any
other means, I had a shot-board[44] nailed over the hole, and made
as water-tight as possible. While we were digging the ice out of the
ship, I had already determined that the other two holes we had
drilled through the hull were plugged with ice.

Now I did all this to find out whether or not the ship was still
serviceable. For if she were foundered, we could save or prolong
our lives only by getting to the mainland before break-up, as our
boat was too small for us all and was stove in besides. And our carpenter by this time was beyond all hope of recovery, and there was
no one else to complete the pinnace. But worst of all, there were
not more than four of us strong enough to travel over the ice
through the deep snow, so miserable was our condition.

On the 25th one of our major worries was over, for we discovered
on that day that the ship was still sound. We discovered this when
the wind again shifted to the north, raising, as it usually did, an
abnormally high tide. We noticed then that, where we had dug down
beside the ship, the water rose more than a foot above the hole in
the hull that we had patched. At the same time the water didn't rise

at all inside the ship. This encouraged us so much that we fell lustily
to work breaking up the ice within the ship and heaving it overboard. At the same time, I set the cook and a few others to thawing
out the pumps. By continually pouring hot water into them, they
had cleared one by the morning of the 27th, and when we tried it, it
delivered a good flow of water. So we set to work and pumped out
two feet of water; then we stopped pumping to determine if the
water level would remain where it was, or if the vessel was leaking.
Thus we continued digging out the ice from our ship, and the next
day, when we had cleared out the second pump, we found that it,
too, was in good working order. We also found that the water was
no longer rising in the hold.

On the 29th it rained steadily, a sure sign that winter was finally
coming to an end. On the 30th we were at work early, although it
was very cold and we had snow and hail, which distressed the sick
men more than any time that year. Next day, May 1st, the weather
was equally bad, and we returned to the house fairly late. There
we built a fire and, endeavouring to cheer ourselves up by any
means, we each chose a lady in far off England and wore her name
ceremoniously in our cap. And because you find us now in this
merry humour, let me tell you that we kept good cheer at Christmas
and Easter; and let me tell you also how we fed ourselves all winter.

When we left England, we were well-provided with beef, pork, fish,
etc., which the cook now prepared in the following manner. The
beef for Sunday night's supper he boiled on Saturday night in a
kettle of water to which he had added a quart of oatmeal. After
boiling the mixture for about an hour, he removed the beef and
boiled down the broth till its volume was reduced by half. This we
called porridge and ate with bread while it was as hot as we could
stand. Following the porridge, we had our customary fish. For
Sunday dinner we had pork and peas, and for supper the beef that
had been formerly boiled, along with some more porridge. In like
manner, the beef for Tuesday was boiled on Monday night, and
Thursday's beef on Wednesday. Thus we had a warm supper in our
bellies every night except Friday. And surely this did us a great
deal of good.

But soon after Christmas, many of the men were afflicted with such
sore mouths that they could eat neither beef, pork, fish nor porridge.
Their diet consisted mainly of bread or oatmeal which they
pounded into flour in a mortar, then fried in a frying-pan with a
little oil. Some would boil peas to a soft paste, and feed as well as
they could on that. For the greater part of the winter water was our
only beverage. And during the whole winter we took not more than
a dozen foxes, many of which would lie dead in the traps for two
or three days before we collected them. These would be unwholesome because the blood would have settled. But if one would be
found alive in the trap, or not too long dead, it would be made into
broth for the sick men who were weakest. The flesh would be boiled
till it was very soft, and eaten also. Some white partridges were
taken, too, but offered us so little nourishment that they are hardly
worth mentioning.

We had three sorts of sick men. Those who were so sick that they
couldn't move or roll over in their beds, but must be looked after
like infants; those who were crippled as it were, with the aches of
scurvy; and finally those who were sick with scurvy, but not yet
crippled. Most of the men had sore mouths and loose teeth. Yet
these sick and weary men had to work. So our surgeon—as diligent
and sweet-tempered a man as I ever saw—would be at work early
in the morning, picking the men's teeth, and cutting away the dead
flesh from their gums. While the surgeon attended to their mouths,
the men would bathe their own thighs, knees and legs with a con-
coction which we brewed from trees, buds and herbs. At one time
or another we tried each of these. First we would boil it in a kettle,
then pour the brew into a small tub or basin which was placed
under the afflicted parts of the limb, and the whole covered with
cloths.[45] The men would be so crippled that they could barely
stand when they got out of bed. Yet after treating themselves with
this brew for half an hour their aggrieved parts would be so molli-
fied that they were able to wade through the snow to get to the
ship, to gather fire-wood and to do the other things that had to be
done. And by nightfall, they would be as sick as they had been
in the morning. Again they must be bathed and anointed, and
their mouths dressed before they sought the comfort of their

beds. Thus did our miseries follow us all through the winter.

As I had always suspected that we would be weakest in the spring, I reserved a tun of Alegant wine against that emergency. By mixing seven parts of water to one part of wine, we made a weak beverage which was little better than water because the wine had lost its virtue through being frozen. The sicker men were also given a pint of undiluted Alegant each day and a little dram of such poor Aqua Vitae as we had, every morning next their hearts.[46] And thus we made the best use  of what we had, according to the seasons.

## May, 1632

The 1st of the month we went aboard early to heave out the ice. But the next day it snowed and blew so hard, and was so cold, that we were forced to stay in the house all day. At that time of year the unexpected cold did so vex the men that they grew worse and worse. If we got them up from their beds now, they would faint, and could be revived only with difficulty. On the 3rd, those who were strong enough went aboard early to heave out more ice. Much of the land was already cleared of snow, with the melt-water collected in small ponds or pools, to which came many cranes and geese. While the others were working in the ship on the 4th, the surgeon and I went off with a couple of muskets to see if we could take a few of the birds for the men who were sick. Never did I see such wary fowl: we could not get near them as they would be frightened off by the slightest movement. Therefore we returned after about two hours, as we could no longer endure walking through the snow and the marshes. I verily thought that my feet and legs would have fallen off, they ached so badly.

On the 6th John Warden, the first mate, died. We buried him that evening on top of a bare hill of sand that we called Brandon Hill,[47] in the most Christian-like manner that we could. The weather continued very cold, freezing so hard at night that the ice that was formed on a pond would support the weight of a man. By the 9th we had located and dug out our five barrels of beef and pork, and had found four butts of beer and one of cider which God had preserved for us. Although it had lain underwater throughout the whole winter, we could not see that it had suffered in any way. And may God make us ever grateful for the comfort it gave us.

On the 10th it snowed, and there was such a cold wind that we couldn't stir out of the house: yet, in spite of the cold, the snow was disappearing rapidly from the land. Early the next morning we were again aboard, heaving out ice. By the evening of the 12th we had cleared all the ice out of the ship, and in the process had located our supply of spare shoes which had been under water all winter. But we dried them out by the fire and put them on. We put our cables back into the hold, and also a butt of wine that had been stored on the upper deck all winter, and was still frozen solid. We then prepared the ship for sinking again when the ice broke up. So far we had not found anything wrong with the ship and therefore hoped that she was sound.

The carpenter, however, earnestly argued to the contrary, saying that she was well bedded down in the sand, and that it was the ice that blocked her defects and was the only thing that kept out the water. He insisted that when she started working in the open sea her seams would surely open. And indeed we could see right through her seams between wind and water. But what troubled us most was the loss of her rudder, and the fact that she was exposed to the full force of the tidal current, which might tear her to pieces when the ice broke up. However, we hoped for the best.

The 13th being the Sabbath, we kept it as solemnly as we could, giving thanks to God for such hopes and comforts as we daily enjoyed. By now the days were beautiful and warm, although it still froze at night, and we could see some bare patches of earth. On the 14th we started a new project. The boatswain, with a party of men, brought ashore the rest of the rigging from the ship. This had been seriously damaged when we hacked it out of the ice, and they now set to work to repair it. I also had the cooper put our casks in order, although the poor man was very infirm. My intention was to pass some cables under the ship and to buoy her up with the casks if if we could not get her afloat any other way. Another group of men

I sent out hunting in the hope that we could take some birds for
the sick men who were growing weaker each day. And it should be
noted, too, that we had no shot for the muskets except what we
made from the aprons[48] of our guns and some old pewter that I had.
For we didn't dare to use the carpenter's sheet-lead.

On the 15th I manured a little patch of ground that was bare of
snow and sowed it with peas, hoping to have some of the shoots to
eat. For as yet we could find no green thing to comfort us. Our
carpenter, William Cole, died on the 18th, a man whose loss was
keenly felt by us all. We missed him both for his innate goodness
and for the present need we had for a man of his abilities. He had
endured a long sickness with admirable patience and died a godly
death. In the evening we buried him beside Mr. Warden. This we
did accompanied by all the men who could walk, for at that time,
three more of our principal men were lying in their bunks expecting
to die within the hour. And thus were we in the most miserable
situation in which we had yet found ourselves.

Before the final stage of his sickness, Mr. Cole had brought the
work on the pinnace to the point where she was ready to be bolted
and trunnelled together to receive her planking. Therefore we were
not so discouraged by his death that we gave up hope of finishing
the pinnace ourselves if the ship should prove unserviceable. Our
pinnace had a keel of 27 feet, a beam of 10 feet and a depth of
hold of 5 feet: she had 17 ground timbers, 34 principal braces and
8 short braces. He had built her with a round stern to save labour,
and she was indeed a fine, well-proportioned vessel of 12 or 14 tons
burden.

After the burial that evening, the master of the ship returned
aboard and discovered the body of our gunner under the gun-room
ports. This body we had committed to the sea a good distance from
the ship and in deep water, almost six months before. On the morning of the 19th, I sent some men to dig out the body. The gunner
was frozen fast in the ice, his head downward, his heel (for he had
but one leg) upward, and the bandage still on his wound. By the
afternoon they had dug him out, and after all that time he was as

free of corruption as when we first committed him to the sea. The
only alteration that had been caused by ice, water and time was that
now his flesh would slip up and down on his bones like a glove on
a man's hand. In the evening we buried him with the others. On that
same day, George Ugganes, who could handle tools better than the
rest of us, had more or less repaired our boat. And so we ended that
mournful week.

By that time, most of the forest was free of snow. Yet when we
climbed a tall tree on the highest point of the island—the one we
called our watching tree—we could see no signs of the ice breaking
up in the bay. The 20th being Whit Sunday, we were mournfully
solemn and ate some wild fowl that were hardly worth the trouble.
The 21st was the warmest, sunniest day yet. I sent two of the men
to see if they could shoot some birds, and with the master, the
surgeon and one of the men I went into the forest with muskets and
dogs to see what I could find. We wandered as much as eight miles
from the house, and although we searched with great diligence we
could find nothing edible, not an herb or a leaf. And our hunters
had no better luck. In the woods much of the snow was gone, making them passable. While the ponds were almost free of ice, the
bay in every direction was frozen solid.

The snow on the island does not melt away with the sun and rain
and cause floods as it does in England; it is simply sucked up by the
sun till it is full of holes like a honey-comb, and the ground under-
neath the snow will not even be damp. We also observed that there
were never any floods, no matter how hard it rained. When we
went aboard the ship on the 22nd, we found that she had taken on
so much water that it had risen above the ballast, again making us
question her soundness. We manned the pumps and pumped her
completely dry. By now it was so hot during the day in the shade
that we didn't dare go out in the sun; yet everything froze at night.
Such weather tormented the men who were now growing weaker
each day.

On the 23rd our boatswain, who had been sick for a long time,
and who had resisted his sickness manfully, was attacked by such a

pain in his thigh that we truly thought he was about to die. So
great was his illness that he stayed in bed all day. And it was a
maxim among us that if a man stayed in bed for two days he would
never get up. This made every man strive to be up and around. The
24th was a very warm, sunny day. Along the shore the ice was disappearing and all over the day it cracked with a fearful noise.
About three in the afternoon, we could see the ice moving past the
ship with the ebb-tide. I immediately sent two men to tell the master
to unstop the hole in the hull and thus sink the ship, and also to
look for the rudder through the cracks in the ice. This he presently
performed. Then a lucky fellow, David Hammon, prodding between
the ice-floes, struck the rudder with his lance and raised it to the
surface of the water. When he yelled that he had found it, the rest
of the men came running and pulled it up on the ice and then into
the ship.

Meanwhile, carried by only a slight current, the ice began to pile
up in great heaps against the shoals and rocks, and also against the
heap of ice that we had placed as a barricade to protect our ship.
Although the drifting ice did us little damage, we were forced to cut
off 20 fathom of cable that was frozen in the ice. After an hour the
ice stopped moving, as there was no place for it to go, everything
outside being frozen. That was indeed a joyful day for us all, as it
gave us hope, for which we gave thanks to God. The 25th was a
fine, warm day, and with the ebb-tide the ice crashed against the
ship and shook her viciously.

On the 26th I again went wandering through the bush with the
surgeon. We also went to the bay where we had lost John Barton
through the ice last year, but could find no trace of his body or
anything else. By the 28th there was almost no ice between the ship
and shore, and I thought we were out of danger, so I had the men
plug up the lower hole in the hull. At that time there was three feet
of water above the ballast.

As the 29th was the birthday of Prince Charles, we had a holiday,
and displayed His Majesty's colours both on land and aboard ship.
That day, too, we named our tiny settlement Charles Town or by

Plate 7  Entrance to Salt Water Lake, where one of James' men drowned

contraction, Charlton, and the island Charlton Island. We launched
our boat on the 30th, and for the first time were able to go to and
from the ship by water. And the next day, the last of the month, we
found some vetches[49] growing on the beach. I had them picked
and boiled up for the men who were sick. That same day we finished
rigging the ship, and as it was very hot we dried out our fish in the
sun, and aired all of our other provisions. Except for the master
and myself, there was not a man left among us who was still capable
of eating our salt provisions, so bad was the scurvy. Yet it should be
noted that none of us had been troubled that winter by any rheums
or phlegmatical diseases.[50] Throughout the month the wind had
been variable, but mostly from the north.

## June, 1632

The first four days of June we had constant snow and hail with a
very high wind. It was so cold that all the ponds froze over, and
even the cans of water in the house were frozen. And our clothes
that had been washed and hung out to dry did not thaw out all day.
It continued blowing very hard on the 5th, with the wind broad on
the ship's beam, which made her roll and wallow in her dock, and
shook her up badly even though she was sunk. In addition, the ice
was pounding against her, giving her many fearful blows. I decided,
nonetheless, that we would attempt to hang the rudder, and when
God should send us water, to move her off the shoals in spite of
the abundance of ice that was still around. In the afternoon we followed a small cable which was attached to an anchor which lay
astern in deep water, and with some difficulty raised the anchor.
The cable had lain slack under the ice all winter, and this was the
first time we had enough open water to raise it. Its long immersion
had caused it not a bit of damage.

I put some of the men to making colrakes[51] so that they might go
into the water and rake a hole in the sand to let down the rudder.
On the 6th, we set about hanging it. Our lustiest young men took
turns going into the water to rake away the sand from the stern of
the ship. But the water was so mortifying that they could scarcely
endure it for more than five minutes. We finally brought the

rudder to the stern-post, but were forced to abandon the project because of the cold. So we plugged the upper holes in the hull and again fell to pumping her out. We tried to hang the rudder on the 7th but were forced once more to abandon the project. We put out anchors with slack cables so that we would be ready to heave her in position when she started to float. By the night of the 8th, the ship was pumped dry and was afloat, although she was still embedded almost four feet in the sand.

After much discussion, I decided to heave out all the ballast, hoping that the water-logged bilges would be heavy enough to keep her upright. If that didn't lighten her sufficiently to get her out of the sand  I would cut her down to the lower deck, take out her masts and buoy her off with barrels. We started work on the 9th, early in the morning. We hoisted out our beer and cider, rafted the kegs and fastened them to the anchor cable. Presently the beer and cider sank to the bottom, which didn't surprise us, as we knew that any wood that had been under the ice all winter would sink if it was heaved overboard. That day, we also heaved out 10 tun of ballast.

And now I must remind you of God's goodness towards us in sending us those green vetches that I mentioned earlier. For even the sickest man, those who for the last two or three months could not have bestirred themselves even if their lives depended on it, were now up and around. The other men were also getting stronger, and it was wonderful to see how rapidly they recovered. Twice a day, we went to gather the herb or leaf of the vetches as they first appeared out of the ground. After they were washed and boiled, we ate them with oil and vinegar that had been frozen. It was an excellent and refreshing sustenance, and most of us ate nothing else. Sometimes we would crush them and mix the juice with our beverage; some-times we ate them raw with our bread.

On the 11th, a very warm day, we finally hung the rudder. The tides now were very deceptive. Even a north wind raised very little water, which made us fear that we might never get our ship out of the sand. On the 13th, after a careful examination of the instru-ments, and after practising for two weeks, I worked out the latitude

of Charlton and found it to be 52° 2′ north. By the 14th we had
heaved out all the ballast and carried ashore all the yards and other
heavy items, so that the ship was now as light as possible. On the
15th we did very little besides taking some exercise, for by that
time even the most feeble had grown stronger and could run about.
The flesh of their gums had become healthy again, and their loose
teeth were now fastened so that they could eat beef with their
vetches.

That day I went to the tree which we used as a watch-tower and
found that in every direction the sea was still frozen solid, while
our bay was dotted with pieces of floating ice which had no way
of escaping. As the 16th was outrageously hot with some thunder
and lightning, the men went swimming in one of the ponds which
they found to be still very cold. Lately there had appeared a variety
of flies, such as butterflies, butcher-flies and horse-flies, and such
an infinite abundance of blood-thirsty mosquitoes that they
tormented us more than the cold had ever done. I think that they lie
dead all winter in pieces of old, rotten wood and then revive again
in the summer.  There was also an abundance of ants upon the land
and of frogs in the ponds. These we did not dare to eat because they
were speckled like toads. By this time there were neither bears and
foxes nor fowl to be seen—they had all gone.

When the wind shifted to the north on the 17th, we expected a
high tide. Early in the morning, therefore, we returned to the ship
and ran a small cable astern through the gun-room port, but the
tide didn't raise the water even a foot. In the evening, by watching
some stones that I had placed as markers, I saw that the water
was beginning to rise rapidly. I signalled for the boat to come
ashore, then took all of the able-bodied men on board the ship.
Although she had not risen completely clear of her dock in the
sand at high tide, we manned the capstan and heaved with such
energy that we winched her through the sand and into water that
was a foot and a half deeper. I didn't dare to take her farther out
because there was still too much ice around. After she was moored,
we knelt in prayer, thanking God for giving us back our ship.

We were up early on the 18th—the cooper, with some assistants, to
fill the casks with fresh water, myself, with another group, to pile
up stones at low tide. The coxswain with his crew, ferried the stones
to the ship at high tide, where the master and the rest of the men
stowed them away. At low tide, the vessel had a sharp list to the
offing which enabled us to plug more firmly the two upper holes in
the hull. Later we prepared other convenient places where we
could drill holes to sink her if the occasion arose. The next day
we were again up early, continuing with the same tasks. For the
last two days the ship had been grounded, so it was a happy occasion when she floated off on the highest tide we had yet seen on the
island.

In the evening I climbed up to our lookout and for the first time
could see some open water apart from the small patch by the shore
where our ship was moored. The sight of some open water was
very comforting, because it suggested that break-up was not too
far away. We continued our labours on the 20th, with the wind
at north northwest. The tide rose so high that day that our ship was
afloat, so we drew her farther off till she had a foot and a half of
water under her keel. Thus we moved her little by little into deeper
water, because the ice was still perilously thick around us. On the
22nd much ice was driven about and against us, so that we dragged
our stern anchor. In spite of the ice all around us, we heaved the
ship farther off at high tide so that she she might remain afloat even
at low tide.

During the next low tide, we took soundings all around the ship
and found that the bottom was very foul. We found stones rising
three feet out of the bottom, and two of them within a ship's breadth
of the vessel itself. Thus were God's mercies made manifest to us.
For had she struck one of those stones when we were forcing her
ashore, she would surely have stove in her bilges. We could now
see that there were many such dangers in the bay because of the ice
that was grounded upon them. In the evening we towed the ship
to the spot where she had been anchored last fall. There we moored
her, and day and night and flood and ebb, we sheered the ship
amongst the dispersed ice that came athwart of us.

The 23rd we continued to fetch our provisions aboard. To do this, we were forced to wade through the water the distance of a bow-shot to reach the boat because a south wind had lowered the water-level in the bay. That morning, I observed the meridian transit of the moon by a meridian-line that was 120 yards long, and had been rectified many weeks beforehand.

I had formerly cut down a very tall tree and made it into a cross. I now fastened to the cross pictures of Their Majesties, the King and Queen, doubly wrapped in lead so tight that they were protected from the weather. Between the pictures, I affixed His Majesty's royal titles, viz., Charles I, King of England, Scotland, France and Ireland; also of Newfoundland and of these territories and to the westward as far as Nova Albion,[52] and to the northward to the latitude of 80° etc. On the outside of the lead I fastened a shilling and a sixpence of His Majesty's coin; under that we fastened the King's arms, fairly cut in lead, and under that the arms of the City of Bristol. And it being Midsummer Day, we raised the cross on the top of the bare hill where we had buried our dead companions. By that ceremony, I formally took possession of those territories to His Majesty's use.

The wind, continuing from the south and blowing hard, pushed so much ice upon us that we were in great danger of losing the ship. Flood and ebb we laboured with both poles and oars to heave the ice away from the vessel. But it was God who finally protected and preserved us. For it was beyond the understanding of any man how the ship could endure such punishment or how we, by our labour alone, could have saved her. During the night the wind shifted to the westward, blowing the ice away and letting us finally have some rest.

On the morning of the 25th, the boatswain and some of the men began to rig the ship while the other men continued to ferry provisions aboard. About ten o'clock, when it was getting dark, I picked up a lance and with one of the men carrying a musket and some fire went to our lookout tree to build a fire on the highest point on the island to see if it would be answered. I had previously built such fires to find out if there were any savages on the mainland or the islands around us. Had I located any, my purpose was to contact them to see if there were any Christians in the area or any intelligence of an ocean sea thereabouts. When I came to the tree, I laid down my lance, and my companion laid down his musket. Then, while I climbed the tree I ordered him to set fire to some low tree thereabouts, and he inadvertently started his fire to windward. Because the weather had been extremely hot, all of the vegetation was dry and sere, and burned like flax or hemp. When I saw that the wind was blowing the fire in my direction, I hurried down from the tree. But before I was half way down, the fire attacked the bottom of my tree and blazed so fiercely upward that I was forced to leap from the tree and dash down a steep hill to escape being burned. On the ground the moss was as dry as flax and the fire would run strangely along the earth like a train of gun-powder. The musket and the lance were both burned. My companion finally located me and was surprised to see that I was not burned. And thus we went homeward together, leaving the fire burning most furiously and spreading rapidly. For we could do nothing about it.

That night I got little sleep, and at daybreak I sent all our powder and beef aboard the ship. Then I went back to the hills to see what was happening with the fire and found it burning most furiously both to the west and the north. Leaving one man on a hill to watch it, I hurried home and had the men take down our new suit of sails and carry them to the shore where they could be thrown into the water if it became necessary to preserve them. I also had the men start immediately to take down the houses. About noon, when the wind shifted suddenly to the north, our sentinel came running home with the news that the fire was following hard on his heels like a train of powder. No one needed to tell us to hurry everything to the shore: for the fire came towards us with a most terrifying, rattling noise, and was a full mile in breadth. By that time, fortunately, we had removed the sails that covered our houses, and were carrying our final loads to the boat. Then did the fire come to our town, seize it, and in a trice did burn it to the ground.

We lost nothing of any value in the fire, for we had already carried

everything to a safe place. During the conflagration, our dogs
would sit down on their tails, howl, and then run into the sea.
Finally the wind shifted to the east, driving the fire to the westward
where it looked for new things to devour. That night we were all
together aboard the ship and thanked God that He had preserved
her for us.

The 27th, 28th and 29th we worked hard at fetching our gear
aboard. We also loaded our water, which we had to tow off with the
ebb, and float to the ship on the flood. Moreover, we had to go
around the eastern point to collect driftwood, for our tools were so
worn out that we couldn't cut any. Therefore I had had our pinnace
sawn up into fire-wood some three days earlier, together with some
old casks which I also broke up. At low waters, and such other
times as we could not work in carrying things aboard, I had the
men fetch stones and build tombs over our three dead companions,
filling up the spaces with sand in a decent and handsome fashion.
The smallest tomb had two tons of stones about it.

The 30th we bent on all sails and by eleven o'clock at night
everything was in order. Our plan was to finish our work by the end
of the month so that we might celebrate the Sabbath more solemnly
on shore the next day, and so take leave of the island where we had
wintered. The wind had been variable then for a good while, and
the bays were completely free of ice—it had all gone to the northward. Hoping that it will please some readers, I will now relate
the manner in which the ice is broken up. First, it must be noted
that it does not freeze naturally above six feet. Any ice that is
thicker has been piled up by accident. But such ice may be as much
as six fathom thick. This was proved when we were digging the ice
out of the ship and digging out our anchors before the ice broke up.

In May, when the heat of the sun increases, the ice thaws first in
the shoal waters along the shore. Then the tidal currents—as well
as the rising and falling—place such a strain in the main ice that
it cracks and breaks up. As soon as there is room for it to move
about, one piece of ice rides upon another, and it is so bruised
and ground upon the shoals that it is broken into smaller and

smaller pieces till a ship can pass through it easily. Besides this, much of the ice is stranded on the shoals where it is consumed by the heat of the sun. At this place spring is most unnatural. In the daytime it will be extremely hot, with the sun almost unendurable because of the glare and reflection from the sand; yet at night an inch of ice will form on the ponds and on tubs of water in the house. And all this, towards the end of June. By the time we left the island, the mosquitoes were almost intolerable. We tore up old cloth and made bags to put our heads in, but even this didn't protect us. They still found ways and means to sting us so that our faces were swollen with pimples which so itched and smarted that we could not stop scratching them. And those flies and insects tormented us more than all the cold that we had previously endured.

**July, 1632**

Because the first of the month was a Sunday, we were up early. I had our ship decorated with what we had—our standard at the poop and the King's colours at the main-top. I had prepared a short narrative of all our passages on this voyage to the present, together with a statement as to our current situation. I also pointed out that I intended to explore both to the south and to the west of the island. I concluded the brief narrative with a request of any traveller who might take it down or happen to notice it to make our labours known to our sovereign lord the King. And thus with our arms, drum and colours, we went ashore, cook and kettle, marching first to the lofty cross near which we had buried our dead companions. After reading morning prayers, we strolled up and down till dinner time. After dinner, we walked to the highest hills to see which way the fire had burned, and saw that it had consumed everything to the westward for at least 16 miles. Because they were on a bare hill, neither the cross nor the graves of our dead had been touched by the fire.

After evening prayer, I happened to be walking along the beach when I found an herb resembling scurvy-grass.[53] I had some picked and boiled with our meat for supper. It was most excellent—far better than the vetches we had been eating. After supper, we

gathered two bushels of the scurvy-grass which we later found very
refreshing. And when the sun was set, and the boat came ashore
for us, we assembled ourselves together and went up the hill to take
a final look at the tombs of our dead. Resting my hand on one of
the tombs I uttered some lines which the wise may find shallow,
but which nevertheless moved my young and tender-hearted companions to some compassion at the time. These were the lines:

I were unkind, unless that I did shed,
Before I part, some tears upon our dead.
And when my eyes be dry, I will not cease
In heart to pray, their bones may rest in peace.
Their better parts (good souls) I know were given,
With an intent they should return to heaven.
Their lives they spent, to the last drop of blood,
Seeking God's glory, and their countries good.
And as a valiant soldier rather dies,
Than yields his courage to his enemies,
And stops their way, with his hew'd flesh when death
Hath quite deprived him of his strength and breath.
So have they spent themselves. And here they lie,
A famous mark of our Discovery.
We that survive, perchance may end our days
In some employment meriting no praise.
And in a dunghill rot. When no man names
The memory of us, but to our shames.
They have out-liv'd this fear, and their brave ends,
Will ever be an honour to their friends.
Why drop you so, mine eyes? Nay rather pour
My sad departure in a solemn shower.
The winters cold, that lately froze our blood,
Now were it so extreme, might do this good,
As make these tears, bright pearls which I would lay
Tomb'd safely with you, till doomes fatal day.
That in this solitary place, where none
Will ever come to breathe a sigh or groan,
Some remnant might be extant, of the true
And faithful love, I ever tender'd you.
Ah, rest in peace, dear friends, and let it be
No pride to say the sometime part of me.
What pain and anguish doth affect the head,
The heart and stomach, when the limbs are dead.
So griev'd, I kiss your graves, and vow to die
A foster-father to your memory.            Farewell.

So wrapping my brief securely in lead, I fastened it firmly to the
cross. Then presently we climbed into the boat and left, never again
setting foot on that island. The island, like the others around it, as
well as the mainland, is composed of a fine, white sand, covered
with a white moss, and dotted with shrubs and low bushes. Some of
the hills and some other patches are free of vegetation, and there
the sand will drift like dust before the wind. The island is also thick
with trees such as spruce and juniper, but the biggest tree that I
saw was only a foot and a half through.

When we first arrived on the island, we saw some deer and managed
to kill one, but never saw any more. All through the winter we saw
many foxes and killed about a dozen of them, but in May they all
disappeared. We saw a few bears and didn't manage to kill any of
them; we also saw some other little beasts. In May some ducks and
geese arrived, but we killed very few. A few white partridges were
also seen, but we had no shot left to hunt them with. And we never
saw a fish in the sea or a fish-bone on the shore. We saw a few
cockle-shells but they were empty. Anything else worthy of note
I have already mentioned.

Plate 8  Parkland in interior of Charlton Island

# Our Exploration and Coming Home, July, 1632

Monday being the 2nd of July, we were up early, stowing our gear, putting things in order and weighing our anchors. When the last anchor was raised, we knelt in prayer, beseeching God to continue his mercies to us, and thanking him for having thus restored us. We found that the ship was sound; we still had plenty of the provisions which we had brought out from England and we were in fairly good health and getting stronger by the day. Thus we weighed anchor and came cheerfully to sail. As the wind was in the northwest, a very bad wind for us, we stood over to Danby Island to take on more wood, and to wait for a more favourable wind. I went ashore myself with the boat because the men told me that the previous year they had seen some stakes driven into the ground there.

When we landed, I went to the place where the men reported seeing the stakes, while they gathered up driftwood along the shore. I found two stakes, each driven into the ground about a foot and a half, and some ashes and charcoal where a fire had been made near them. When I pulled up the stakes, which were about the thickness of my arm, I found that the ends had been sharpened to a point with a hatchet or some similar iron tool. It appeared, too, that they had been driven into the ground with the head of the same iron tool. They were about a stone's throw from the shore, and I couldn't fathom what purpose they could have served unless it was some mark for boats. Finding the stakes increased my desire to locate some savages, for without doubt they could have told us of Christians with whom they had traded.

About four o'clock in the afternoon, I returned aboard with a boat-load of wood. As the wind was now more favourable, we weighed anchor and, with our lead, tried to find a channel through those perilous shoals. In the evening the wind again shifted to the north-west, and we anchored between Charlton Island and the island I had named Carie's Island last fall in memory of that honourable gentleman of the bedchamber, Mr. Thomas Carie. We spent the night at anchor there. At daybreak on the 3rd, we weighed anchor, and with a light breeze sounded up and down looking for a chan-nel. Many times we were in only four or five fathom of water; then when the wind increased, we stood away to the west, till at noon nothing was visible to the north but ice. Attempting, therefore, to swing around the westernmost point of Charlton Island, we hoped to seek a passage to the southward but found it to be all shoals, rocks and reefs.

By four in the afternoon, we could see the mainland to the west, all choked with ice; and as the wind favoured us, we stood to the northward, keeping the mainland in sight. The 4th was calm and so foggy that we couldn't see a pistol-shot in any direction, so we rode at anchor all that day and the next night. On the 5th, at three o'clock in the morning, we weighed anchor but there was so much ice around us that we knew not which way to turn. Now, to avoid relating the same event 20 times over, I will summarize: till the 22nd, we were so pestered and tormented by the ice that the very telling of it seems incredible. Sometimes we were so blinded by fog that we couldn't see about us. As we became more determined in our endeavours, we would strike the ship against the ice with such violence that the cook and the others who were below would come running to the deck, thinking the ship had been beaten to pieces. Indeed, we struck so many unavoidable blows against the ice every hour that we finally left the hatches open so that 20 times a day the men could go down into the hold to see if the bilges were stove in.

Sometimes, when we had moored the ship to an ice-floe for the night, a violent storm would break our cables and beat us from one floe to another most fearfully. At other times we were stuck fast in

pack ice that rose as high as our poop. This was caused, as I
mentioned earlier, by one slab of ice riding up on another, till, on
occasion, the pile would draw eight or ten fathom of water. On
occasion the bottom slab of such a pile would become dislodged
and strike us under the bilges, a slab that might weigh as much as
eight ton. Many times we had to pump clear water for over an hour
before the vessel was dry. In the midst of these several and hourly
dangers, I overheard the men muttering that they would be happy
if I were in my grave. For they were certain that we were destined
to starve upon some lonesome slab of ice. I was forced to endure
all this with patience and to comfort them when I found them in a
better humour.

The 22nd we were vexed with a storm all night and in the morning,
in a thick fog, we drifted into 13 fathom. About noon it cleared,
and we saw land. At the same instant, we had a good observation
which showed that we were at Cape Henrietta Maria. I had the
master stand in towards the land, and meanwhile we made a cross
to which we fastened the King's arms, and the arms of the City of
Bristol. When we anchored in six fathom, about a mile from
shore, we hoisted out the boat, took our weapons and our dogs and
went ashore. We erected the cross upon the highest spot we could
find.

On looking around, we saw a great many deer and set to stalking
them with all the skill we had. We even set the dogs on them, but
to no avail, for the deer ran away from them at their pleasure. All
that we did was to tire the dogs and weary ourselves. Nor could
we get close enough to shoot them, although I saw about a dozen—
old and young—that were very goodly beasts. By wading into the
pools, we took half a dozen young geese, then we returned very
vexed to our boat: for we had found a place where there was a
good supply of fresh meat, and yet we could not get it. Up to that
time we had kept the dogs aboard ship with a great deal of incon-
venience all winter. We had also pardoned them many misde-
meanours (for they would steal the meat out of our steeping tubs)
in the hope that they would be of some service in the future. When
I learned that they were of no use to us, and would not be in the

future, I left them there. They were a dog and a bitch, buck-dogs
of a very good race. The dog had a collar around his neck which
may come to light in the future. I saw no signs of any savages,
nor could we find any herb or other refreshing thing.

When I returned aboard in the evening, a fair south wind was
blowing, so I had the master weigh anchor and set sail immediately
in the hope that we would find open water to the northwest. The
cape had a very shoal point in the offing which we hoped to get
around. Sailing, therefore, amongst shattered ice, we came to very
shoal water—four and five fathom deep—which we could not
avoid. As we stood to the north, the water gradually deepened, but
it brought us also amongst great slabs of ice which were grinding
together on a fairly heavy swell caused by some open water. Those
solid slabs of ice made a most terrifying noise, but it proved to be
a fair, moon-lit night, otherwise we would have been in trouble. We
turned amongst that ice, stopping the ship sometimes within her
length of huge slabs as dangerous as rocks. Because we were often
forced to bear up, we were pushed to leeward almost upon the main
body of ice. So we let fall an anchor and all stood on the deck to
watch the ice's sheering of the ship. Although we had poles and
oars to fend off the ice, we could still not keep clear of it, and many
pieces came foul of us. We broke two of our large poles at this
work, poles that were made to be handled by four men, and suffered
some other damage besides.

At daybreak we weighed anchor and tried every possible means to
get clear of the ice, but it was impossible. I believe it would be
impertinent to relate every particular day's passage, as to us they
were very much alike. Our labours were sometimes with our sails,
but still, in that ice, we gave and got 500 fearful blows a day. When
we could find a little open water, we would ride at anchor, giving
the ice a chance to drift to leeward. At other times we would be
completely trapped in the ice, and it would break, rise and leap up
under us till we expected hourly to be pounded to pieces. Moreover, we would have such storms in the dark of night that the
cables which moored us to an ice-floe would be parted. Then we
would spend the rest of the night pounding most dangerously on

one floe after another till daylight when we could see to make her
fast again. I won't speak of the thick fogs which we had daily and
which froze our rigging day and night. Besides all that, we then
came upon most uncertain depths—20 fathom, then 10, 15 and 9,
with a foul, rocky bottom.

In addition, the thick slabs of ice drifting through those uncertain
depths did so distract the tides and so confuse our reckoning that
by the 30th we had been driven both to the east and the south of
the cape. At five o'clock in the evening the cape bore northwest of
us and was some three leagues off. With all that mischief, our ship
had now become so leaky that we had to pump her out every two
hours. At that point I called a consultation, and after reviewing
our previous experience, we were all of the same opinion: it would
be impossible for us to get to the northward or the eastward because
of the ice. Therefore, I resolved as follows: when the wind blew
from the south, it would blow the ice offshore, and we would try to
get to westward between the shore and the ice. I must confess that
this was a desperate resolution, for we knew the whole coast to be
most foul, littered with rocks and stones. Therefore, if the wind
would shift to the north, there would be little hope for us apart
from God's mercies. But where we were we could not stay, for the
nights were growing long, and the cold was becoming so severe that
the sea was beginning to freeze between the pieces of ice. I had
the ship put in readiness and had convenient places prepared to
sink her for the second time, should we be forced to such
extremities.

When the wind shifted to the south, we put our plan in execution,
moved around the shoals off the cape and then stood in towards
shore to get between it and the ice. We came into four fathom, over
a very foul and rocky bottom, hoping to spend the night at anchor
while the ice drifted to leeward. But there was still so much
ice between us and the shore that we were forced to stand further
into the ice to attain deeper water and let the ship drift with the
pack. As the wind was increasing, we spent a dark and dangerous
night. In the morning, we set to work to get the ship out of the ice
and into some clear water that we saw to the west by south. Some

of the men climbed out on the ice to heave the ship forward with their shoulders, while others stayed aboard with poles. The rest were busy working the sails. By nine in the morning, we were out of the ice, standing west and by south in four fathom of water over a foul bottom. Because we were unable to weather some large, drifting ice-floes, we were forced to stand off again, and drop our anchor when it grew dark.

About midnight a large floe which we couldn't avoid came athwart our cable and made the ship drag her anchor. This drove us into shoal water, with many rocks and a foul bottom. We attached the cable to the capstan and heaved with such heartiness that we dragged the anchor from under the ice and on to the ship. Thus we tried, as best we could, to keep ourselves in eight or ten fathom of water. It then pleased God that the wind should blow along the shore, otherwise we would have been in even more trouble.

The 1st of August, at daybreak, as soon as we could see where we were, we again started to struggle with the ice, trying to get nearer to the shore. Then, because the wind was against us we dropped the anchor, hoping that the ice would drift to leeward and leave the sea clear of ice to the west. But the ice became very thick about us, with one chunk fouling our sprit-sail yard which made the ship drag her anchor till we were able to fend it off. So we weighed anchor and stood in closer to shore. But the water shoaled rapidly, and there were so many large ice-floes between us and the shore that there was no safe anchorage, so we turned again into the ice. Many pieces of that ice were aground on the shoals, and few of the pieces were even a cable-length apart. That day we saw two wal-ruses on the ice.

We were very glad to see daylight on the 2nd, having spent a most dangerous night amongst the ice, and having endured many a heavy blow. So we stood in again to the shore to see if we could find some open water, for to the north was nothing but impassable ice. We stood into five then four fathom, but still there was nothing but ice, so we stood off again into deeper water till by evening we were once more enclosed among monstrously large cakes of ice. As we were in a very thick fog, also, we lashed the ship to a large, flat piece of ice and went to sleep to refresh ourselves after our extreme exertions.

The 3rd, 4th and 5th we were surrounded by large ice-floes, and at the same time were caught in a bad storm. When we tried to work our way to the westward, we struck such heavy blows against the floating ice that the whole bow of the ship would shudder. But if we stopped pushing her and simply let her drift with the pack, then pieces of ice would break off and rise under the ship, leaving us in an equally dangerous position. The ship took on at least a ton of water during every watch, and we had to pump this out in addition to our normal labour. May God think of us and be merciful to us amongst all these dangers.

At noon on the 5th we were at 55° 30′ north, with the cape bearing southeast by east, some 12 leagues off. And that is all the distance we had covered since the 22nd of July. All night we had a violent gale from the west northwest; about midnight, when we were made fast to an ice-floe, our hawser parted and we lost 14 fathom of it. We pounded fearfully all night, being tossed from one chunk of ice to another, because I didn't dare to send the men out on the ice to make us fast in the dark for fear of losing them. The storm lasted all through the 6th and again drove us almost back to the cape.

The 7th was the most comfortable day we had experienced since we left our wintering place. The wind was fair at east, and although we still suffered inconveniences and dangers, we got into open water near shore and covered many leagues to the westward. Moreover, the leak in our hull now stopped of its own accord, so that now we rarely had to man the pumps. We sailed all night, keeping a sharp lookout from the forecastle, and bearing up for one watch and luffing off for the other. We continued thus on the 8th also, till the wind shifted to the northwest, driving the ice on the shore and forcing us to anchor in eight fathom. The main body of ice was some two miles to windward, but the set of the tide kept it from us. At noon our latitude was 55° 34′ north.

In the evening a large slab of ice drifted down upon us, making us
weigh anchor and stand in closer to shore, where we anchored in
six fathom. About midnight, when the wind increased, the ship
started to drift. Soon we were in five fathom where we dropped the
sheet-anchor which finally stopped her. But we were still in trouble,
for if the main pack of ice should drift down upon us, there would
be no hope but to put the vessel ashore. On the morning of the 9th,
we weighed our second anchor when the ice was within less than
a mile of us. About eight o'clock, a piece of ice came afoul of us,
but we escaped injury by moving to a new anchorage in three and
a half fathom.

As the wind continued from the north northwest, driving us on a
lee shore, I had all of our empty casks filled with water and the
ship left unpumped. I also checked the places where we had
decided to drill through the hull should it again become necessary
to sink her. For we were then in as great danger as we had been
at any time during the voyage and, to our grief, were on a foul,
rocky bottom. The problem was that if we made fast to a piece of
ice that drew a lot of water, as soon as it grounded on those rocks,
it would shatter and betray us to our destruction. About noon we
became fouled on the point of an ice-floe, but instead of giving
way we decided to ride it out at anchor, thinking we might break
through it into some open water which we could now see. As we
were thrusting and fending with our poles, a huge piece of ice came
athwart our hawser, and on a rolling sea the ship fell upon it so
violently that I expected she would have stove in her bows. At
length, the ship drifted with the ice so that I thought our hawser
had parted. But when we heaved it aboard with the winch, we
found that the sheet-anchor was broken off in the middle of the
shank.

So we set our sails, hoping to claw off that perilous shore and get
in amongst the ice. It pleased God to favour our plan, for by eight
o'clock that night we were off into seven fathom. Then, as a dark
night was coming on, we made fast to the largest piece of ice we
could find. All night there was a fair amount of wind, but about
midnight it shifted to the north, driving us closer and closer to shore.

By daybreak on the 10th, we had been driven into four fathom of
water, where the bottom was so foul that the lead would fall off
rocks that were three or four feet high. So we set our sails and tried
everything we could think of to edge away from that terrible shore.
Some of us climbed out on the ice to line her forward, while others
stood by with poles to fend her off. By dark, we had worked her into
eight fathom and had made fast to the highest piece of ice we could
find. You are probably wondering why we kept so near the shore
when that was so obviously dangerous. We did that because the ice
was so extremely thick in the offing that there was no possible way
to get through it. Moreover, if we were caught in that huge ice-
pack, when a fair wind came up from the south, southeast or east,
we could not get out of it. Therefore, we chose to run the risk and
to prevent or overcome all hazards with God's assistance and our
extreme exertions.

On the morning of the 11th, there was an east wind in spite of a
thick fog, so we stood in towards the shore. From the 11th to the
14th, the wind continued fair, so day and night we carried as much
sail as the ice would safely permit. In the daytime, we had the shore
in sight on our port side and the ice within two miles to starboard,
while we sailed among scattered floes, luffing off for one and
bearing up for another.

By noon on the 14th our latitude was 57° 55′ north. And by that
evening we were embayed in the ice so we stood to the southwest
to get clear of it, but were unsuccessful. When we saw from the
mast-head that there was open water beyond the ice, we headed into
it, but by nightfall we were in very thick fog which forced us to tie
up to a slab of ice to wait for daylight and better weather.

Although the fog was still very thick, we stood away to the west
the next morning to get out of the ice. Within two hours, however,
the water shoaled from 40 to 25 fathom which told us that we
were approaching the western shore of the bay. So we swung around
to the northward in a fog so thick that we could not see a pistol-shot
in any direction. When we had sailed on this course less than two
hours, we heard the growling of ice ahead of us—a most hideous

sound. We hauled our tacks aboard, standing to the westward; in the semi-darkness caused by the fog, we would sometimes see the ice and sometimes only hear it, but it was composed of large chunks rising high above the water. However, we weathered it all except a few small pieces and finally got into open water.

About sunset, there came a sudden gust of wind from the north northwest, and we barely had time to trim our sails. It continued gusting till nine o'clock when it grew into a most violent storm. We considered what might be our clearest course, then took in all her sail, letting her drift with her head towards the shore. Before midnight, when the water shoaled to 15 fathom, we turned eastward, and set our main course on a lowered yard so as not to expose too much sail. The water deepened but a little, and we knew that we were on the same rocky shoals which we struck last year. God be merciful to us! For this was the first great breaking sea we had seen that year.

On the morning of the 16th we were driven towards a large ice-floe, and to avoid it set our fore-course too and stood towards the shore till we were in 13 fathom, then stood to the offing again. We continued about a mile into the ice, but a great swelling sea made our position unendurable, so we stood out again. The storm broke up about three o'clock in the afternoon with the wind settling down fair in the northwest, which helped us as we had not moved for four hours; besides it was but two leagues between the shoals and the ice. We set all our sails and endeavoured to weather the ice but it was still pestering us in the evening. By midnight we didn't know which way to turn, nor what to do, so we took in all our sails and let the ship drift with the ice. This beat against us on every side as there was a heavy sea running.

The next morning, the 17th, as soon as it was light, we saw that we were still surrounded by ice. But the storm had broken the ice into irregular chunks as big as a boat of three or four tons which dealt us many heavy blows in the night. If that storm had taken us deeper into the ice it would have beaten us to pieces, but for God's miraculous preservation. So we set our sails, hoping to get clear

of it to the northward, which we did by eight o'clock in the
morning. We then knelt in prayer, thanking God that he had
delivered us from our perils, for we had been in the jaws of death,
so to speak, during every hour for a space of six weeks. Never
have I heard of anyone enduring such long nights on such a foul,
shoal coast, and tormented with ice as we were. At noon our
latitude was 58° 20′.

Now regarding the melting of this ice, we found that the storm
had shattered only the edge of the pack, and would have taken
a long time to break up the main body of ice. During July and
early August, I took some of the ice into the ship where I cut it into
a two-foot square and put it into the long-boat. There, in spite of
direct sunlight, the warmth of the ship, where we kept a good hot
fire, and all our breathing and movement, it was still not melted
after eight or ten days. It was our practice when we were moored
to a piece of ice to set up marks so that we could measure its rate of
melting: this yielded us small hope that the ice would ever dissolve,
for in the time we had we never saw it grow smaller, or float lower
in the water. Nevertheless, I think that in some years the ice is
broken up by storms or consumed by the sun, or else the bay would
be frozen solid. But I confess that these secrets of nature are beyond
my comprehension.

Being out of the ice—though we could still see it clearly to the
eastward, even from the deck—I ordered the master to steer away
to the north and by east, following the shoaling of the western shore.
At noon on July 18th our latitude was 59° 30′ north. On the 19th
we continued our course between north northeast and north by
east till noon, when we were at 61° 07′ north and some 12 leagues
off shore. Then I ordered the master to shape his course to the
northeast and to head for a spot between Carie's Swan's Nest,[54] and
Ne Ultra.[55] On the 20th, when our latitude was 61° 45′ north, we
saw a few seals around the ship. The 21st the water shoaled so
much that we thought we were approaching land, but about noon
the wind shifted to the northeast where it was dead against us. We
luffed as close to the wind as we could, and as it increased we stood
to the east and the east by north.

On the 22nd we made land-fall to the west of Carie's Swan's Nest, where we had 40 fathoms of water at three leagues off. So we stood in to within a league of shore where, in 13 fathom, we could see land to the south of us. As we swung around it we could see that it was Carie's Swan's Nest, which lies at 52° 00′ north.[56] All of the 23rd we sailed northeast, and for the most part in sight of land. The 24th, at noon, I estimated our latitude to be 63° 30′ north, having sailed a northeast course. Most of the day there was a very thick fog, though it cleared a bit around one o'clock so that I expected to see land. I saw nothing, but some of the men with sharper eyesight than mine spotted land about two leagues away. I knew that it could only be Nottingham Island, though that was contrary to the expectations of our best mariners. As we stood in closer to shore to make certain, we saw that it was indeed Nottingham Island, with its north end bearing due east.

At that point I ordered the master to steer northwest by north. All of the men were reluctant to carry out my order because of the thick, foul weather, but they finally submitted. The reasons for my decision were as follows: because of the lateness of the season, the fact that winter was almost upon us, I wished to follow the shortest path through lands that had already been explored. If I found an open sea, I would have achieved my objective, and intended, then, to proceed with everything in my power; on the other hand, if I did not find an open sea—that is, if I ran into land—my exploration would be finished, and I would return home.

We set what sail we could in the very stiff breeze that was blowing; then, about eight in the evening, the wind freshened to a gale, so we furled our top-sails and stood under our two courses and bonnets. By nine o'clock, the wind had become increasingly violent from the south southeast, so we took in our fore-sail, and let her drive northwest. The storm continued all night with extraordinary violence, forcing us to heave the lead every two hours. But the ship was moving so fast that she would be past the lead before there was 20 fathom of line out. In addition, the night was exceedingly cold.

On the 25th the storm continued with such malice and perplexed us so seriously that few of us either ate or slept for 24 hours. About six o'clock in the afternoon, the storm began to weaken, although there was still a fierce gale blowing from the south and southwest. We were standing west northwest when suddenly the sea became very smooth. We tried to comprehend what might have caused it and decided that it must be the leeward tide. We saw nothing afterwards that made us question our decision. The ship moved very rapidly through that smooth water.

On the 26th, about two o'clock in the morning, we were suddenly in the ice: but it pleased God that at the moment the moon should be bright enough for us to see what was happening immediately around us. We would have hove to, but the ice was so thick to windward and so close to us that we didn't dare. We then bore up in this unexpected accident and I truly believe that two or three times we missed the ice by less than a foot. Then we stood to the eastward, close to the wind, waited for daylight so that we might see. From the mast-head, we could see ice to the north northwest, the northwest and all the way around through the south to the east. There was even some ice to leeward. The ice was in large, solid cakes, with the sea between them as smooth as a mill-pond.

This whole situation made us very disconsolate, so I called a consultation with my associates: namely, Arthur Price, master; William Clements, lieutenant; John Whittered, master's mate; Nathaniel Bilson, surgeon; and John Palmer, boatswain. I asked them to advise and counsel me on how we might act most effectively. The men consulted together, then brought me their written opinion, which read:

Our advice is that you repair homeward this day—August 26th, 1632—and for these reasons: first, the nights are long and so extremely cold that we can hardly manage the sails and rigging.

Second, this is the season of stormy and windy weather, such as we are having now. As it has been storming continually since the 24th, this is not the time to go exploring.

Third, we doubt that Hudson's Strait is sufficiently clear of ice that we can pass through it before it freezes up. For winter is fast approaching, and the sea is already thickly sprinkled with ice-floes.

Fourth, we must have a spell of fair weather to get through the strait, and we may have to wait a long time if we neglect the first opportunity.

Fifth, our ship is leaking so badly that in foul weather we are forced to pump every half hour, which is a great strain on us all. Moreover, she is so sorely bruised with pounding on rocks and blocks of ice, that she should no longer be sent among them, but should save our lives by sailing homeward. And besides all this, our men grow very weak and sickly with such harsh labour.

Sixth, the season is so far advanced that we can expect no improvement in the weather. That is, we will continue to have snow and fog which will freeze our rigging, and make everything so slippery that a man can hardly stand. And this weather we have with a south wind. Should it shift to the north, we can expect far worse.

Seventh and last, the way we must go is choked with thick slabs of ice as all men here may see.

And therefore we hereby counsel you to return homeward, hoping that God will give us a favourable passage, and return us safely home if we proceed calmly and do not tempt him too far by our impatience.

Indeed, most of their reasons were obviously sound, and I could not say anything to contradict them, or suggest any way that we might proceed with our exploration. And so with a sorrowful heart (God knows) I agreed that the helm should be born up, and a course steered for England. I hoped that His Majesty would judge my endeavours graciously and forgive my return. We set out to discover populous kingdoms and to take special notice of their magnificence, power and policies, to bring home samples of their riches and commodities and to pry into the mysteries of their trade and commerce. But we discovered no kingdoms, populous or otherwise. Nor did we fight great battles against the enemies of God and our country. Yet do I hope that our willingness to explore in those desolate regions may be acceptable to our readers.

When we bore up the helm, our latitude was at least 65° 30′ north, and we were northwest and by north from Nottingham Island.

Some of the men thought that we were actually farther to the northward, but as our latitude was by dead reckoning rather than by
observation, I chose to record the lesser figure. On the 27th the
wind shifted around to the northwest and would in any event have
prevented further exploration in that direction. In spite of the
wind the sea was fairly calm, so that by noon we were athwart Cape
Charles—that is, between Cape Charles and Mill Island. The
previous night had been very cold, with a heavy snowfall, so that
all our rigging and sails were frozen, and all the land was covered
by a blanket of snow. And now, since I mentioned formerly that it
snows very much, it might not be out of place to consider the
reasons for this.

When I was upon Charlton Island, where we spent the winter, I
often looked to see if there was any dew on the grass. I did this in
June when there was virtually no snow on the ground, and sometimes following the hottest days. But I never observed any dew,
although little was to be expected from moss and sand. So that
which was exhaled from the snowy ice and the cold sea was simply
returned to earth in the same form. Thus we continued generally
on our course, blinded by fog and dirty weather that was blended
with snow and frost, steering between scattered pieces of ice that
on occasion rose higher than our mast-top. With a great variety of
winds, we were also driven within three leagues of both shores, so
that the last of the month we were in the narrowest part of the
strait, which is about 15 leagues across, the south shore being
seriously pestered with ice.

## September, 1632

The 1st and 2nd, we continued fighting our way eastward. As the
weather cleared up in the evening of the 3rd, we sighted the
southern end of Resolution Island. Those three days and nights had
been so extremely cold, with fog and frost, that the men could
hardly take in our top-sails and sprit-sail. We had previously sailed
through much mountainous ice, far higher than our mast-head, but
that day we sailed by the highest that I had ever seen, which is
incredible indeed to relate. Then, as the wind shifted to the east,

we felt a new swell, an ocean swell that made the ship work with
a different motion than she did with any wind or swell that came
from the west. From the 3rd to the 8th, we had a variety of winds
that pushed us clear of the straits. The weather was foul and gusty
one minute and calm the next, while there was such a turbulent
sea that I thought the rolling of our ship would pitch her masts
overboard. This made the vessel so leaky that we were forced to
pump every half hour. Even the deck seams were open, so that
we were soaked in our beds.

That was the last day that we saw any ice. As we now had favouring
winds, we hurried homeward with all possible haste. During my
unfortunate voyage, I had carried out many experiments and made
a number of observations, which I organized on the way home. As
I was subsequently ordered to publish my observations, I most
submissively offer them now to the judicious reader. I also present
my personal opinion regarding the feasibility of the intended
activity—to find a northwest passage into the south sea. The merest
echo of some tales regarding Portuguese explorers who came here
out of the south seas have come down to us, but I leave that story
to be confounded by its own vanity. That story, however, occasion-
ally excited some of our more active spirits to search for that purely
imaginary passage. For mine own part, I give no credence whatever
to those absurd stories, and as little to the Portuguese and Spaniards
of a later date; these never mention such difficulties as shoal water
and ice, or even the sight of land, but sound as though they had
been carried home in a dream. And indeed, their discourses are
found to be absurd, and their charts (by which some of them have
tried to deceive the world) are mere fabrications, with water
where there should be land and land where there should be water.

One thing, however, is certain. The northern parts of America, to
the latitude of 80° and upwards, have been discovered only through
the industry of our own nation. And this has been so carefully done,
through the labours of several different men, that the supposed
passage must lie to the north of 66°, for south of that the mainland
has all been explored. North of 66°, however, is a region of extreme
cold, pestered with ice and other hazards, which the Spaniards

could not long endure because of their dispositions and their weak
speeke-ships.[57] And in addition, it is known that the entrance to
Hudson Strait is but 15 leagues wide, with the middle much nar-
rower, and between Salisbury Island and the mainland the strait is
only 8 leagues wide. Proceeding then to the northwards, to 66°, it is
but 15 leagues from shore to shore. In length this strait is about
140 leagues, as will appear more plainly on the map [Map 3, p. 26].
It is, in addition, most infinitely pestered with ice until August and
some years cannot be navigated even then. In fact, I don't think
that the strait is ever completely clear of ice.

In all probability, there is no northwest passage to the south sea.
I make this statement for the following reasons:

First, there is a constant tide, flood and ebb, setting into Hudson
Strait, with the flood coming from the eastwards.

Second, there are no small fish such as cod, etc., in the strait, and
very few large ones. Nor are there any bones of whales, sea-horses
or other large fish to be found on the shores, nor any driftwood.

Third, we found the ice in the latitude of 65° 30′ north to be lying
all over the sea in huge floes, and I am most certain that the shoals
and shallow bays are the mother of it. Had there now been any
ocean beyond it, it would have been broken all to pieces such as we
found going through the strait, and into the ocean to the eastward.

Fourth, the ice drifts to the eastward, leaving the bay through
Hudson's Straits. This I have often observed both from Resolution
Island and from sailing through the ice in the strait.

Now if there is a northwest passage to the south sea, we know that
over a distance of 140 leagues, it is quite narrow in several places.
In addition, it is infinitely pestered with ice, as has been reported
by everyone who ever sailed these waters. Now we have some observations taken at Bantam, Gulolo and Firando in Japan, and we
also know the distance between Japan and the west coast of California. If we compare these data with the observations made at

Charlton Island (and refer them all to the meridian of London),
then the distance between the meridians of Cape Charles and the
coast of California will be about 500 leagues. And that is at 66°
north, where the meridians incline very sharply together.[58]

It should be noted, too, that around Cape Charles the variation of
the compass is 29° west, which suggests that there is a large land-
mass in that direction. The supposed strait, therefore, must be very
long. And the only time that it could be navigated is during August
and September, when the nights are so long and the weather so cold
that it is insufferable. In addition, the large ships that are suitable
for carrying merchandise cannot withstand the ice and other hazards
without placing themselves in very great danger. It is easier, too,
to sail 1000 leagues to the southward, around the Cape of Good
Hope where the winds are constant, than 100 in these seas where
you run the daily risk of losing both your ship and your life. And in
these quarters there is nothing to comfort the sick or to refresh
the men. In late August and September, the weather breeds an
infinity of storms, and the winds incline to be westerly, so that there
will be little hope of a passage.

Even if the strait were wider and free of ice, what advantage would
be gained by using this passage when the winds are so contrary?
To Japan, China and the northern parts of Asia, it may be the
shortest route: yet the longer route, around the Cape of Good Hope,
is well known, is faster, involves less hardship and is much safer.
Also, to the East Indies and other parts where we have the greatest
commerce and employ the most shipping, the other route is not
any longer. What commercial benefits might be obtained from a
shorter route to northern Asia I will not presume to say. But I am
sure that there is a great difference between the northern parts of
Asia and the northern parts of America, for there are certainly
no commercial benefits to be obtained in any of the places I visited
during this voyage.

We arrived in Bristol Road on the 22nd of October, having been
held up by tempestuous weather and contrary winds. When we
brought the ship into harbour and hauled her up on shore it was

found that her cut-water and stem had been torn and beaten away,
together with 14 feet of her keel. Much of her sheathing had been
cut away, her bow was broken and bruised and many of her internal
timbers were broken. And under the starboard bilge, a sharp rock
had cut through the sheathing and planking, and penetrated an
inch and a half into a timber. There were so many other defects,
besides, that it was miraculous how the vessel could ever have
brought us home.

On our arrival at Bristol, we all went to church where we gave
thanks to God for having preserved us in the face of so many
dangers. I know very well that what I have hastily written down
here will never discourage any noble spirit from attempting to
settle, finally and forever, the quest for a northwest passage to the
south sea. And it is probable, also, that there are navigators who
have a better understanding of the problem than I have myself, as
well as a sounder method of seeking its solution. To them I wish
every happiness and success. And if all they do is to review what has
already been done, and to bring back more accurate celestial
observations and hydrographic descriptions, or improve the practice
of northern navigation, it will be a most commendable undertaking.

I have now wasted several of my mature years in procuring useless
information from foreign nations, but have also visited many different learned people of this kingdom for their instructions. I have
bought everything I could find in print or manuscript, and every
chart or paper pertaining to the search for the northwest passage.
I gave my time voluntarily, both to preparation and exploration,
as well as in writing this narrative of the voyage. In addition, I
spent £200 of my own money in the above endeavours and in
supplying some special items for the expedition. And I have no
regrets. For I take a great deal of comfort and pleasure from the
fact that I am now able to give a fairly reasonable account of those
parts of the world that had never before been described to my
satisfaction.

## The Copy of the Letter which I Left at Charlton Fastened to the Cross, July 1, 1632

Be it known to anyone that shall happen to arrive here on this Island of Charlton that our Sovereign Lord, Charles I, King of England, Scotland, France and Ireland, Defender of the Faith, etc., did desire to find out whether or not there was a northwest passage through these territories to the south sea. Therefore, some of the members of the Worshipful Company of Merchant Adventurers of the City of Bristol decided to satisfy the desire of His Majesty. So they voluntarily offered to fit out a ship for that purpose, well-manned, victualled and furnished with everything else that was required. His Majesty not only commended their offer, but graciously accepted it. Whereupon they fitted and furnished forth a ship called the *Henrietta Maria,* of 70 tons burden, victualled for 18 months. The number of people thought convenient to manage such a venture was 22 men—19 carefully selected seamen, 2 boys and my unworthy self, their commander. The Bristol merchants most judiciously and bountifully supplied everything, and had all arrangements completed by the 1st of May, 1631.

We began our voyage on the 3rd of May. We stood out of the road of Bristol, commonly called King's Road, passed Cape Cleere in Ireland and sailed along many courses which added up to west northwest. On the 4th of June we raised Greenland to the north of Cape Farewell, where we were trapped in the ice for two days, and were in great danger. When we got clear of the ice, we doubled Cape Farewell to the southward and then continued to the west, pushing the ship through much ice.

On the 19th of June, we reached Resolution Island. While we were

trying to work around it to the south, a strong westerly wind sprang
up, pushing the ice on the shore, and the ice, in turn, pushed us
ashore. In that distress I sent the shallop to sound out a place of
refuge for the ship but as soon as it was gone, it was in the same
situation as we were and could not return to the ship because of
the ice. As we had been driven very near the rocks by this time,
we were forced to set our sails and push the ship into an opening,
risking her among unknown perils in order to avoid obvious perils
before we could moor her in a place that we thought would be safe.

On June 22nd, the ice which virtually filled the inlet was piled so
high by the ebb-tide that the normal course of the tidal current was
deflected towards the ship and, in spite of all our efforts, drove
her upon the rocks. As the water ebbed away, the ship hung by her
keel upon a rock and heeled to the offing. As soon as we perceived
this, we rigged some hawsers to her masts and to the rocks to hold
her upright, but to no avail. She heeled over farther and farther
as the tide continued to fall, till she was at such an angle that we
couldn't stand upright. At that point we all climbed out onto a
piece of ice, looked at our sorry ship and prayed that God would be
merciful to us. The rock that the ship was perched upon was
just abaft the main-mast which made her hang after the head, and
she sank over so much that the gunwales of the forecastle were
under water. But at last the tide turned when it was still a foot
higher than the previous tide, or the following tide, thanks be to
God, and the ship rose safe and sound. And thus we were miraculously delivered.

With the first wind, we proceeded to the westward. We were
pestered with so much ice, however, that it was about the middle
of July before we reached Sir Dudley Digges Island. And there, I
had to make a decision, for I had been ordered specifically to
explore two areas: first, to investigate to the northwest of Digges
Island, and if that were not feasible, then second, to go to the
Checks[59] and Hubbart's Hope, and search from there to the south-
word. But we already found ourselves seriously pestered with ice
at 64° north, and as far as we could see to the northward there was
more ice. It was also so late in the season that before I could get

very far to the northwest it would be late August, and I would have to return, with equal difficulty, to Digges Island. By that time the year would be so far advanced and the nights so long and cold, that I would probably be forced—to my shame—to return to England.

I therefore stood to the westward towards Mansfield's Island, on which I landed twice, still pestered and obstructed by the ice; then I continued to the west, hoping to find open water in the bay. We were more troubled with ice in the bay, however, than at any place we had previously visited. So it was August the 11th before we sighted the western mainland, which we raised at 59° 30′ north latitude, somewhat south of the Checks. Because of ice and head-winds, we could not sail north to our destination, but we did observe the tidal current and found by later experience that it flowed from the north.

We coasted southward along the shore, staying in sight of land and in 10 fathom of water, till we entered the inlet which was formerly called Hubbart's Hope. This was the very place where the passage to the south sea should be according to the men of England who were supposed to be the best-informed in such matters. We sailed to its very bottom, into three fathom of water, and found that it was a bay some 18 or 19 leagues deep. From there, we continued southward, in sight of land most of the time. As a small gale was blowing, and the sea was running fairly high, I took continuous soundings in 8, 9 and 10 fathom. Then, even before the lead was up, the ship struck a flat rock while she was carrying her fore-sail, fore-top-sail, main top-sail and sprit-sail; she shuddered as she struck three more times, then cleared the obstacle safely. When we passed that danger, we continued following the coastline till we passed Port Nelson.

Finding that the land trended eastward at this point, we started a more detailed exploration, because no one that I know of had ever before visited this land. We stood into six and then five fathom, for it is very low land, and trends for the most part east southeast and east by south. On the 27th of August, I went ashore and in the name of the Merchant Adventurers of Bristol, took possession of the

the land for His Majesty, naming it The New Southwest Principality
of Wales. I took from the land some small trees and herbs and
killed several different kinds of fowl, which I brought back to the
ship as a token of our possession.

Not long afterwards, when we had been pushed back to the westward by contrary winds, we met Captain Fox in one of His
Majesty's ships. Like ourselves, Captain Fox was looking for the
northwest passage. I invited him aboard, entertained him with such
fare as we had taken in this newly discovered land and told him
what we had accomplished. He, in turn, told us us of his discoveries.
He said that he had just come from Port Nelson, where he had
assembled a shallop, and found many things that had been left there
by Sir Thomas Button. The next day he stood to the westward and
we never saw him again. He was very well, as were his ship and
all his company.

We continued our exploration to the eastward till, at 55° 06′ north
latitude, we came to a cape which was named Cape Henrietta
Maria. At the cape the land trends to the southward, and we followed the coast, keeping it in sight, till a storm forced us to stand
out to sea. When the storm had blown itself out, we stood in to the
coast again, so that no part of it would be left unexplored, and
followed it to 54° 40′ north. Another storm again forced us out
to sea, where we passed some islands and finally anchored when
we found ourselves in shoal water at 53° 30′. There we stayed for
a few days, shifting our anchorage several times.

Winter was rapidly approaching, with such long and cold nights
that we were forced to spend most of the day looking for a safe
place to spend the night. Our ship, unfortunately, ran aground
among some rocks the size of a man's head, and pounded against
them most horribly for five hours. During that time, to lighten the
ship, we carried some of our gear ashore, so that by the infinite
favour of God, we got her off again. Therefore, we named the island
the Island of God's Favour.[60] But we were still in great difficulties
among all those rocks. Finally, before a gentle southern wind, we
stood to the northward along the eastern shore of the island, looking

for a convenient place to spend the winter. But we were again
assaulted by a violent storm in which we lost our shallop and were
driven in among various dangers. Then, seeing an opening between
two islands, we ventured into it in very foul weather, found it to
be a very good sound, and hence dropped the anchor.

We landed on one of the islands, naming it Lord Weston's Island;
the other we named my Lord of Bristol's Island. Leaving there, we
stood to the south in search of a wintering place, as the season of
exploration was past. And many a time we had to strain our ground-
tackle for dear life among those islands and shoals. On the 6th of
October, we arrived in this bay, which seemed a very likely place
to find a spot where we could moor the ship. But as we searched the
likeliest places, we found the water to be so shoal and the shoreline so rocky that we couldn't get our ship near the shore. We were
forced, therefore, to ride at anchor a league off shore, in three and
a half fathoms of water.

Winter arrived suddenly. The weather was tempestuous, and the
cold became so intense that our sails, frozen in lumps to the yards,
became quite unmanageable. Neither could our only boat move
from the ship because of the weather.

About the middle of October, I had a house built ashore so that
our sick men might be more comfortable. I intended to dismantle
the house if I could find a wintering harbour for our ship some
place else. Because the boat could not be forced through the frozen,
slushy water, I sent some men on foot to explore the island to see
if they could locate some creek or cove—but to no avail. I had
hoped for warmer and less stormy weather, but now the cables
began to freeze in the hawses, and the ship was solidly covered
with frozen spray. In addition, we were forced to shovel the snow
off her decks.

By this time the water was so thick with frozen slush along the shore
that the boat could hardly get near the island. Yet, in spite of that,
when the wind blew from the northwest, it raised a very heavy surf
along the shore and such a heavy sea in the bay that it was impos-

sible to bring the ship aground. Moreover, had she been aground, she would then have been exposed to east, southeast and south winds, as the nearest land in those directions was two leagues away. Thus, we continued at anchor—to our peril. On the 29th of November, the ice surrounded us on all sides so that our ground tackle was useless. It would have driven us out of the bay, and onto some rocks and shoals—where we would surely have perished, except for the mercy of God. He did send us such a warm day, with the wind at the south, that we brought up some sail, hoisted it up with ropes and so forced the vessel aground in shallow water, where she pounded against the bottom all night.

When the storm subsided, leaving the ship quietly aground, we tried to decide what to do with her. Finally, we decided to sink her. But with the next high tide, and before we had any of our provisions ashore, it started to blow from the northwest, and our ship began to pound against the bottom once more. So we carried all of our dry provisions to the upper deck, and bored a hole to sink her. While she was sinking, however, she was pounded so unmercifully that we thought she would surely be destroyed. When the ship settled so low that the water rose to the upper deck, we all went ashore in the boat. We were so covered with ice and frost by the terribly cold weather, that the sick men who were already ashore couldn't tell one of us from the other.

The next day, we started to land our dry provisions such as bread and fish, during which the men had to wade into the water up to their waists. It was most lamentable to behold. Within two days, the large ice-floes that surrounded us were frozen firmly together into one firm sheet that stretched from the ship to the shore. Thus we were forced to carry everything on our backs from the ship to our house, a distance of about a mile. In a few days, everything in the hold was frozen so solidly in the ice that we could not get anything more out of it. We simply had to leave it there till it thawed out the next summer.

We then built two other houses. The original structure was the house we lived in; the second was a kitchen and dining-room; while

the third was a store-house which we built some distance apart
because of the danger of fire. When that was done, we discussed
the position in which we found ourselves. We all believed, especially
the carpenter, that our ship could never sail again. But even if
she did survive the winter, it might well prove impossible to move
her into deeper water in the summer when the tides were low.
Moreover, because she was lying in the tidal stream, she might be
damaged beyond repair when the ice broke up, and we would then
be without a vessel to carry us home. The carpenter, therefore,
undertook to build a pinnace of some 12 or 14 tons burden and to
have it ready by spring. Then if we found that the ship was not
serviceable, we could dismantle her, and use her planks to cover the
pinnace. By May, the work was so far advanced that the frame
was ready to be assembled and planked.

But God in his mercy did provide otherwise for us. We endured a
a bitterly cold winter during which it pleased God to visit us with
sickness. It was so serious that by the beginning of May, 1632,
only myself, the master and the surgeon were perfectly healthy, and
a little bit later even the surgeon began to be affected. About the
beginning of April, we started to dig the ice out of our ship, and
had completed the job by the middle of May.

On the 24th of May, the ice began to break up between the ship
and the shore; and about the middle of June we warped our vessel
into deep water and found her to be solid and seaworthy, contrary
to all our expectations. Sometime earlier—about the middle of
May—our carpenter died, and with him all hopes for our pinnace.
Master Warden [the first mate] died on May 6th. Our gunner,
Richard Edwards, had his leg broken at the capstan and then
amputated in August, 1631: he languished till the 22nd of November, on which day he died. These three men lie buried here under
these stone tombs. We lost one other man, John Barton, our
quarter-master, who drowned in the little bay that is three miles
due west of this cross. He was crossing the bay when he suddenly
went through the ice, and we never saw him again.

The two pictures wrapped in lead and fastened uppermost on
139

this cross, are of Charles I and Queen Mary, his wife, King
and Queen of England, Scotland, France and Ireland, etc. Below
that are His Majesty's royal arms, and below that again are the
arms of the City of Bristol. And now we are ready to leave. I intend
to continue our exploration to the westward in this latitude of
52° 03′ and also to the southward, although I have little hope of
success. Should I be unsuccessful there, I mean to hasten to Digges
Island and explore to the northward from there. Having had some
experience with the dangers that have to be faced when sailing
through the ice, shoals and rocks of unknown places, I thought it
necessary to leave this testimony of ourselves and our endeavours.
For God might take us to His heavenly kingdom, and prevent our
return to our native land. Therefore I ask that any traveller who
shall find this, or shall hear of it, should inform our Sovereign Lord
the King's Majesty, and assure His Grace that we cannot as yet
find any hope of a passage this way. Inform him that I do faithfully
persevere in my service, accounting it nothing but my duty to
spend my life in giving contentment to His Majesty, whom I beseech
God to bless with all happiness.

I ask, also, that whoever shall find this letter would inform our
Worshipful Adventurers of all that has befallen us. Tell them, too,
that if we should perish it was not through any want or defect in
ship or supplies. For we have ample supplies of everything for at
least four months, and should it be necessary, we could stretch
them to last for six months. At present I am unable to express my
gratitude except through my prayers. But I heartily beseech God to
pour out his bountiful blessing upon the honest endeavours of the
Merchant Adventurers of Bristol, and to assist them in continuing
their noble actions of this kind. And I solemnly promise that if I
should ever find a similar letter or token, I shall report it according
to such instructions as it contains. So desiring the happiness of all
mankind in our universal Saviour, Jesus Christ, I end.

Charlton, July 2, 1632                                    THOMAS JAMES

# Notes

1 Sir Thomas Roe (1581?–1644) was a statesman, ambassador and diplomat who had travelled extensively in the Near East and Europe.

2 See introduction, p. 9, for a discussion of this matter, and for a possible explanation of what appears, at first glance, to be a clear indication of megalomania in Thomas James.

3 Navigation instruments.

4 These included a letter for the Emperor of Japan.

5 The rhumb-line distance is about 1,206 nautical miles or 402 leagues. The course is 290½°. James' course, west northwest, is only ⅓ of a point off.

6 James usually refers to sea-mammals as either "large fish" or "great fish," and the fishes themselves as "small fish."

7 The island was named after the *Resolution,* one of the ships used by Thomas Button during his voyage of 1612–13. Button's other ship was that incredible vessel, the *Discovery,* that had already been pushed through the Arctic ice by George Weymouth in 1602, and by Henry Hudson on his ill-fated voyage of 1610–11. The distant from the Greenland coast to the south end of Resolution Island at 61° 20′ N. is about 457.5 miles, or 152.5 leagues.

8 An overfall refers to surface turbulence caused by strong currents setting over submerged ridges.

9 Isinglass.

10 By "broken grounds," James simply means an area which has a rough, irregular surface such as a boulder-strewn tidal flat.

11 The "beak" or "beak-head" was that part of a ship that was before the forecastle. It projected from the stem to which it was attached, and was supported by the "main knee."

12 That is, she was resting against the rock with her bow lower than her stern, and with her masts leaning sharply out to sea.

13  By the "change day" James refers to the day of the new moon. The
    hour, half past seven, is the time at which high tide will occur each lunar
    month at that place on the day of the new moon. Each day thereafter,
    high tide will occur 48 minutes later until the cycle is completed at the
    end of a lunar month of approximately 29½ days. Or, as John Davis
    points out in his book, *The Seaman's Secrets*, "There are 29 daies, 12
    howers, 44 minutes between change and change one with another
    through the whole yere."

14  Probably named after Robert Cecil, Earl of Salisbury, who was Secretary
    of State from 1596 to 1608. It was named by Henry Hudson or some
    member of his expedition.

15  Mill Island was discovered by Robert Bylot during his 1615 voyage.

16  Digges Island was named by Henry Hudson after Sir Dudley Digges, one
    of his backers.

17  Nottingham Island was named after Charles Howard, Lord High Admiral
    and Earl of Nottingham.

18  Discovered by Thomas Button in 1613, and named after a relative, Sir
    Robert Mansel, who was treasurer of the navy.

19  *Hubbart's Point,* north of Churchill, Manitoba, on a modern chart, was
    named after Josias Hubart, who visited the area with Button in 1612–13.
    Hubbert's Hope was originally the bay or bight where the Churchill River
    flows into Hudson Bay.

20  The rhumb-line course is west southwest, 170 leagues.

21  Nelson shoals. These, and the Nelson River, were named by Thomas
    Button after Robert Nelson, the master of his ship, the *Resolution.*

22  False fires were blue flares that burned several minutes, and were used at
    sea for signalling at night.

23  James is quite inconsistent here. See, for example, p. 42 *supra.*, p. 136 in
    the letter he left on Charlton Island and his map (p. 26, Map 3).

24  Measured when it is either rising or setting, the amplitude of a celestial
    body is the angular distance between that body and the prime vertical, or
    the line connecting the east and west point on the observer's horizon.
    James apparently found the variation of his compass by comparing the
    compass bearing of a rising or setting body with its true bearing.

25  This is now Bear Island.

26  Named after Richard Weston, first Earl of Portland and Baron Weston of
    Neyland. He was Lord High Treasurer from 1628 to 1633.

27  Lightly twisted hempen rope or cord that has been soaked in a solution
    such as limewater and saltpetre. It is easily ignited but slow-burning.

28  The St. Lawrence. See Map 1, p. 3.

29  John Digby, 1580–1653, was a diplomat and statesman, and the first
    Earl of Bristol.

30  Henry Danvers, Earl of Danby, 1573–1644, was a statesman who was
    appointed a privy councillor in 1628.

31  Old-timers call this harbour the Salt Water Lake. See Plate 7, p. 99.

32  He drowned in Salt Water Lake (see letter, p. 139).

33  Suetonius, quoting Augustus Caesar in *The Deified Augustus,* says that
    Augustus "likened those who grasp at slight gains with possible heavy loss
    to those who fished with a golden hook, the loss of which, if a fish carried
    it off, could not possibly be made good by the catch" (*Lives of the Caesars*
    2.25.4).

34  A cable is 600 feet, or one tenth, approximately, of a nautical mile.

35  Sir Hugh Willoughby (?–1554) was a sea-captain sent by Sebastian Cabot
    to search for a northern passage to China and India. He was lost at sea
    near Kegor, in Lapland.

36  Large containers that were used to hold dry items as opposed to liquids.

37  This could refer either to the bottom layer of barrels or, more likely, to the
    bottom rack on which spare hawsers, cables, etc., were normally stored.

38  A quotation from More's *Utopia.* This must have been a very popular
    book with explorers. Just before his frigate, the *Squirrel,* went down in
    1583, Sir Humphrey Gilbert was exhorting his crew with the same
    passage.

39  Sir John Winter was secretary to Queen Henrietta Maria.

40  The next nine lines of the original text are incomprehensible apart from
    the fact that they are concerned with the piling of wood or brush against
    the ends and sides of the house for additional protection against the cold.

41  Bonnets are strips of canvas that were lashed to the bottom of square sails
    to increase the sail area.

42  Strips of canvas rigged along the sides of a vessel to protect the low,
    exposed waist of the ship.

43  Ground timbers are the portions of the ribs that lie athwart the keel,
    forming the floor of the ship. The staddles are the upper or vertical
    portions of the ribs.

44  This refers to the board that was nailed to the hull of a ship where it had
    been pierced by a cannon-ball.

45  This liquid, taken internally, would almost certainly have cured the men.

46  That is, on an empty stomach.

47  It was named after Brandon Hill near Bristol, England.

48  These were coverings for the touch-holes of the cannon to protect them
    from moisture.

49  *Vicia* sp.

50  That is, colds or other upper respiratory disorders.

51  The instrument used for raking cinders and ashes out of an oven or
    furnace.

52  San Francisco Bay area of California. It was named by Francis Drake who
    landed there in the summer of 1579 to repair his ship and take on wood
    and water.

53  *Cochlearia* groenlandica.

54  At the southern end of Coats Island.

55  That is, Roe's Welcome, west of Southampton Island.

56  This is clearly a mechanical error. It should read 62° 00′ N.

57  Speekes were long iron nails with flat heads. James is referring to ships
    that were fastened with these nails rather than the more common trunnels.

58  The westernmost point on the coast of California is Cape Mendocino, at
    124° 24′ W. The longitude of Cape Charles is 77° 25′ W. The difference
    in longitude, therefore, is 46° 59′, which at 66° north latitude is equal to
    1,147 nautical miles, or 382½ leagues.

59  The spot where Thomas Button raised the west coast of Hudson Bay in
    1612. He named the spot "Hopes Checked" because the discovery of land
    checked his hopes of finding a passage to the south seas. Hubbart's Hope,
    on the other hand, derived its name from the fact that a passage might still
    be found through that bay or bight.

60  This island cannot be located on any chart.